CONFIGURING SERVICE MANAGEMENT WITHIN DYNAMICS AX 2012

BY MURRAY FIFE

ISBN: 1497415942

ISBN-13: 978-1497415942

Preface

What you need for this Blueprint

All the examples shown in this blueprint were done with the Microsoft Dynamics AX 2012 virtual machine image that was downloaded from the Microsoft CustomerSource or PartnerSource site. If you don't have your own installation of Microsoft Dynamics AX 2012, you can also use the images found on the Microsoft Learning Download Center. The following list of software from the virtual image was leveraged within this blueprint:

*   Microsoft Dynamics AX 2012

Even though all the preceding software was used during the development and testing of the recipes in this book, they may also work on earlier versions of the software with minor tweaks and adjustments, and should also work on later versions without any changes.

Errata

Although we have taken every care to ensure the accuracy of our content, mistakes do happen. If you find a mistake in one of our books—maybe a mistake in the text or the code—we would be grateful if you would report this to us. By doing so, you can save other readers from frustration and help us improve subsequent versions of this book. If you find any errata, please report them by emailing murray@murrayfife.me.

Piracy

Piracy of copyright material on the Internet is an ongoing problem across all media. If you come across any illegal copies of our works, in any form, on the Internet, please provide us with the location address or website name immediately so that we can pursue a remedy.

Please contact us at murray@murrayfife.me with a link to the suspected pirated material.

We appreciate your help in protecting our authors, and our ability to bring you valuable content.

Questions

You can contact us at murray@murrayfife.me if you are having a problem with any aspect of the book, and we will do our best to address it.

Table Of Contents

Introduction

The Service Management area within Dynamics AX allows you to track all of your service order contracts and service orders for your customers, will track all of your time and expenses against the service orders, and will also pass along any chargeable items to the receivables department for automatic invoicing to the customer.

Service Management has additional functions as well that allow you to track the items that are being serviced, define the tasks that are allowed to be performed against a service order, and also track the symptoms, diagnosis, and resolution to service order issues, making it a great tracking and analysis tool.

In this book we will show how you can create service agreements and orders, and then how you can use the additional tracking features within Service Management to get a tighter handle on your service orders.

SERVICE MANAGEMENT CONFIGURATION

Before we start creating **Service Orders** and **Service Agreements**, there is a little bit of setup that we need to do within Dynamics AX in order to make sure that everything will post correctly, and so that you don't get any complaints from the system.

Because **Service Management** relies on **Project Accounting** quite a bit for the management of costs and transactions, we sill be skipping around the system a little as we do this, but don't worry, it's really not as much work as it initially seems.

Configure Project Line Properties

The service order lines billing properties are managed through the line properties of the underlying project lines within Dynamics AX. And the project lines properties are controlled through the **Line Properties**. So the before we can configure the projects we need to set up a couple of **Line Properties** for **Chargeable** and **Non-Chargeable** line properties.

Configure Project Line Properties

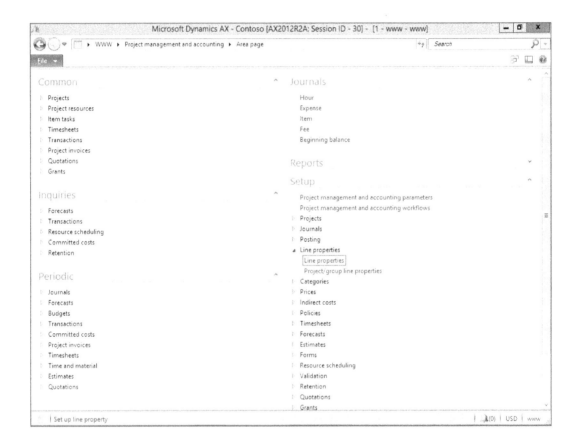

To do this, click on the **Line Properties** menu item within the **Line Properties** folder of the **Setup** group of the **Project Management and Accounting** area page.

Configure Project Line Properties

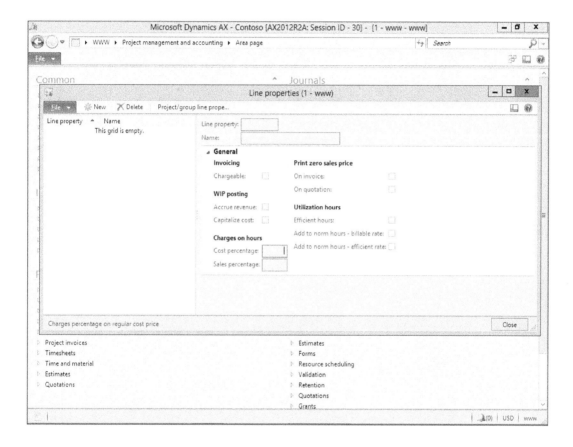

When the **Line Properties** maintenance form is displayed, click on the **New** button within the menu bar to create a new record.

Configure Project Line Properties

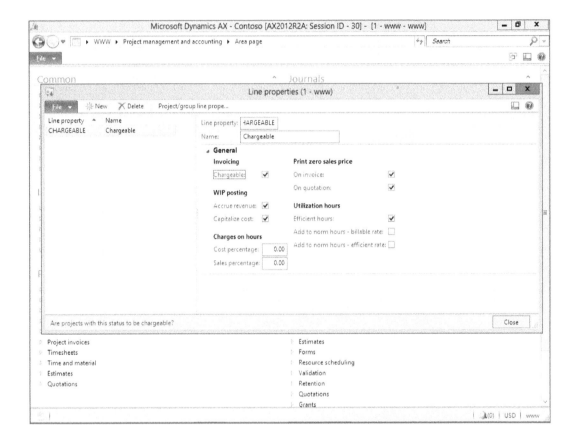

Set the **Line Property** field to **CHARGEABLE** and the name to **Chargeable**. Also, make sure that the **Chargeable** flag is checked for this line.

Configure Project Line Properties

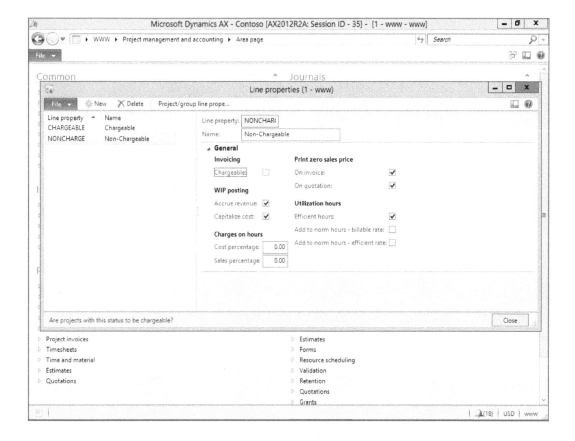

Click on the **New** button in the menu bar to add another record, and set the **Line Property** field for this one to NON**CHARGE** and the name to **Non-Chargeable**. For this record, make sure that the **Chargeable** flag is **not** checked for this line.

When you are done, just click the **Close** button to exit from the form.

Configure A Default Cost Template

Our Service Projects also need to reference a **Cost Template** which will be used to control the hour, expense, and fee costs. So we need to set up at least one default **Cost Template** that we can use later on in the setup.

Configure A Default Cost Template

To so this, click on the **Cost Templates** menu item within the **Estimates** folder of the **Setup** group of the **Project Management and Accounting** area page.

Configure A Default Cost Template

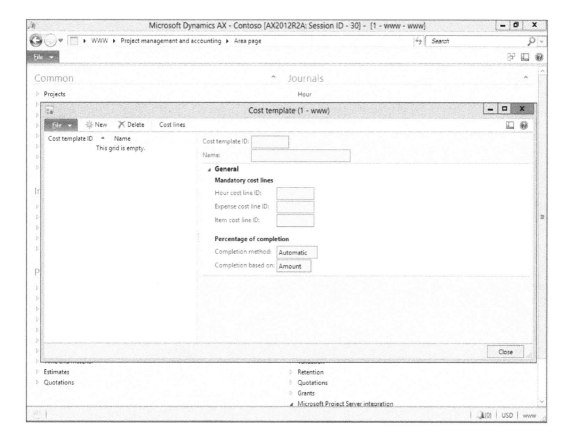

When the **Cost Templates** maintenance form is displayed, click on the **New** button within the menu bar to create a new record

Configure A Default Cost Template

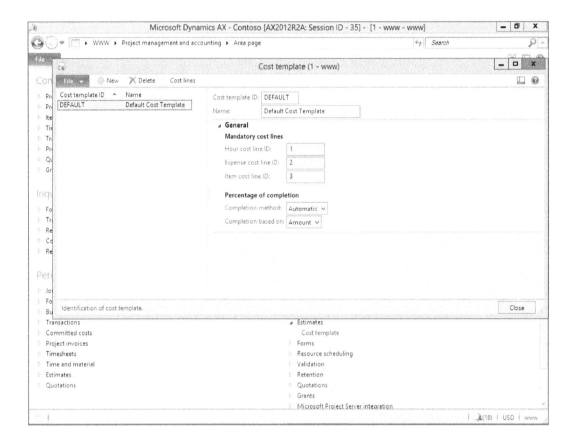

Set the **Cost Template ID** to **DEFAULT**, and the **Name** to **Default Cost Template**. Also set the **Hour Cost Line ID** to **1**, the **Expense Cost Line ID** to **2**, and the **Item Expense Line ID** to **3**.

Configure A Default Cost Template

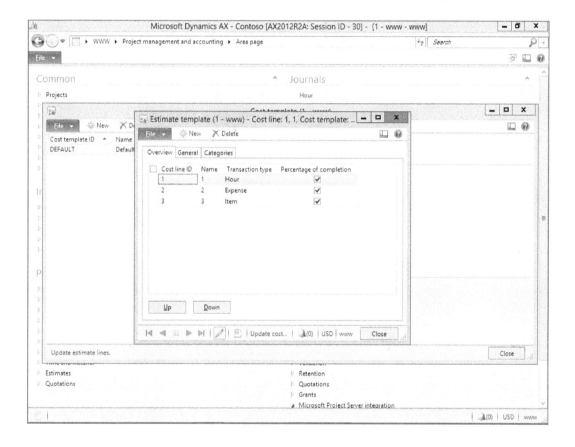

If you click on the **Cost Lines** button in the menu bar, you will be able to tweak additional information about the cost lines, but in this case, you can just accept the defaults, and click on eth **Close** button to exit from the form.

Configure Period Types

The next step that we need to perform is to configure a set of base **Period Types**. These will be used to help us manage the postings that are performed by the Service Management module, and also allow us to control the date groupings of our service orders.

Configure Period Types

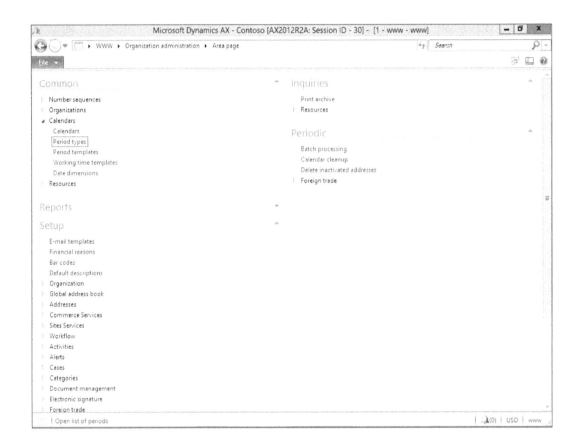

To do this, click on the **Period Types** menu item within the **Calendars** folder of the **Common** group of the **Organization Administration** area page.

Configure Period Types

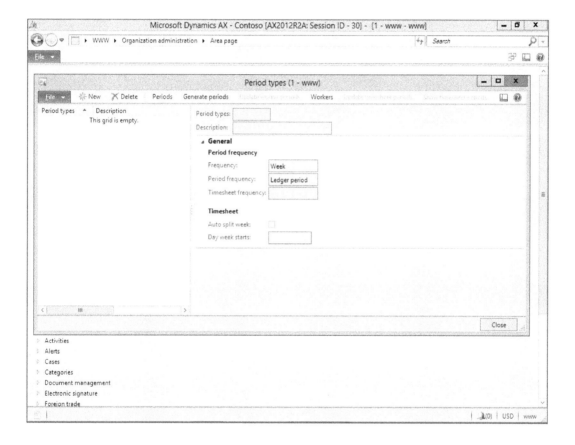

When the **Period Types** maintenance form is displayed, click on the **New** button within the menu bar to create a new record.

Configure Period Types

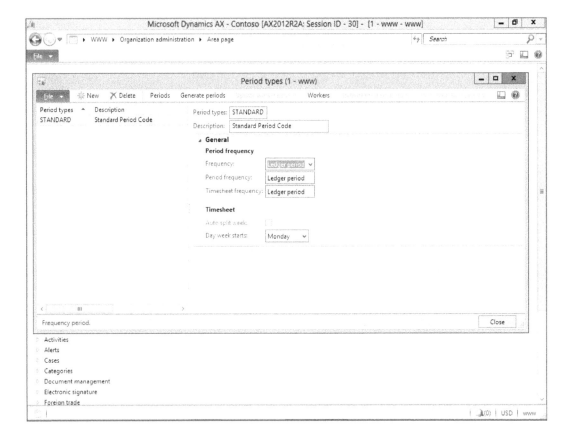

Set the **Period Type** to **STAANDARD** and the **Description** to **Standard Period Code**. Make sure that the **Frequency** field is set to **Ledger Period** and then click on the **Generate Periods** item in the menu bar.

Configure Period Types

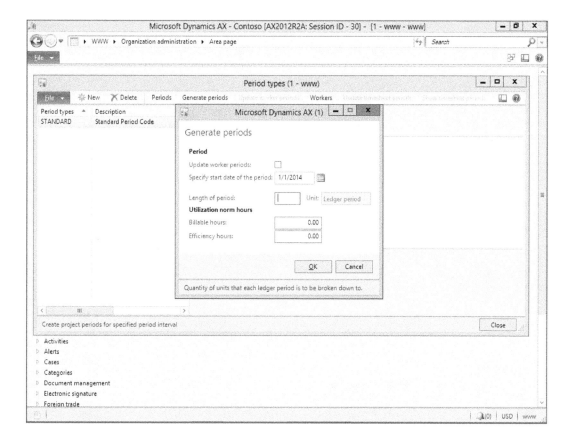

When the **Generate Periods** dialog box is displayed, set the **Length of Period** to the number of periods that you want to create (I usually do enough for a few years) and then click on the **OK** button.

Configure Period Types

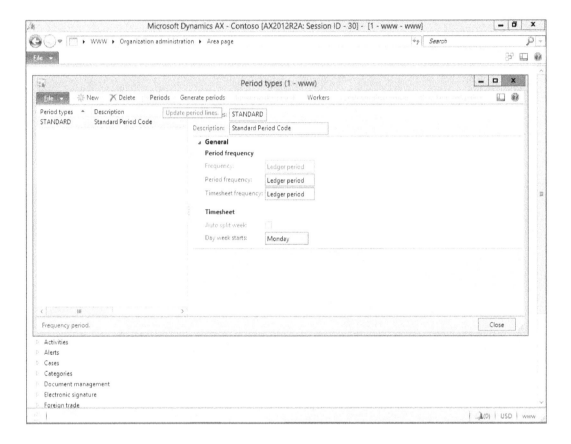

When the process returns to the **Period Types** maintenance form, click on the **Periods** button in the menu bar.

Configure Period Types

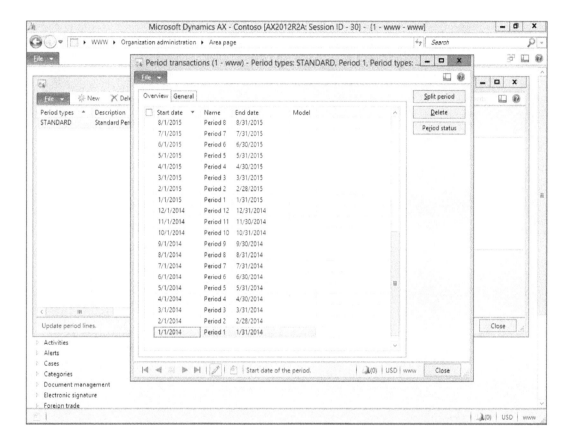

The **Period Transactions** form should be displayed, and you will see that there are a number of periods that have been created for you. You don't need to change any of these values, so just click on the **Close** button to exit from the form.

Configure Period Types

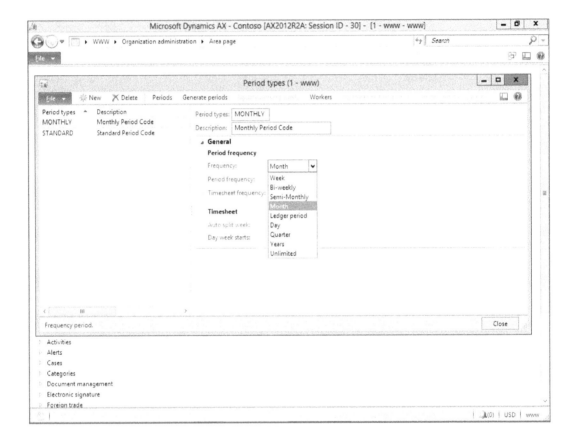

Click on the **New** button in the menu bar to create a new Period Type record. Set the **Period Type** to **MONTHLY**, the **Description** to **Monthly Period Code**. Change the **Frequency** to **Monthly** and then rerun the **Generate Periods** process.

Configure Period Types

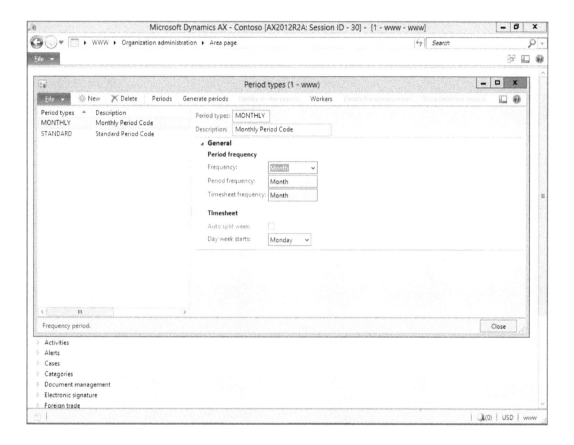

Configure Period Types

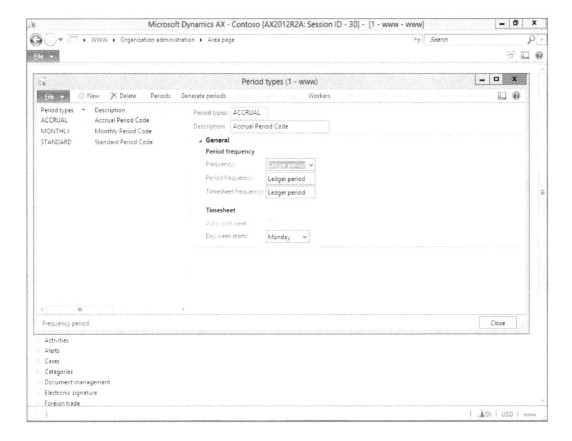

We will create one more **Period Type** for our accrual calculations. So click on the **New** button in the menu bar to create a new Period Type record. Set the **Period Type** to **ACCRUAL**, the **Description** to **Accrual Period Code**. Set the **Frequency** to **Ledger Period** and then rerun the **Generate Periods** process.

After you have done that, click on the **Close** button to exit form the form.

Configure Project Groups

Now we will configure a few **Project Groups** so that we are able to segregate out our different types of Service Orders into groups. This allows us also to segregate the projects themselves that will handle all of the posting of the invoices.

Configure Project Groups

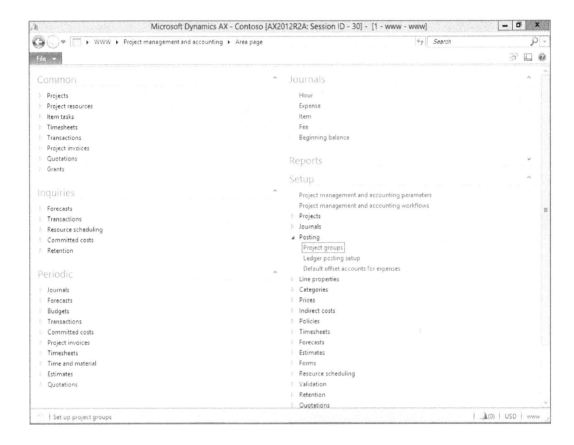

Click on the **Project Groups** menu item within the **Postings** folder of the **Setup** group of the **Project Management and Accounting** area page.

Configure Project Groups

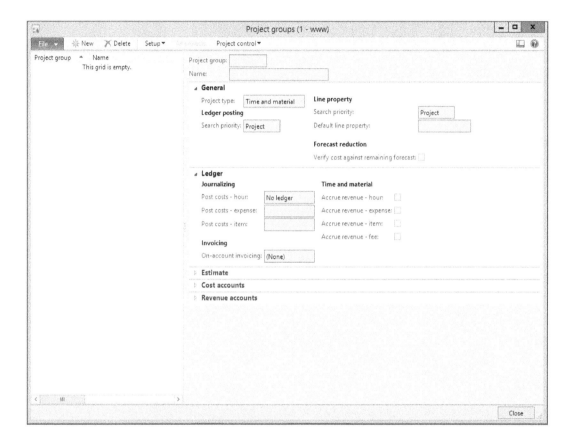

When the **Project Groups** maintenance form is displayed, click on **New** button within the menu bar to create a new record.

Configure Project Groups

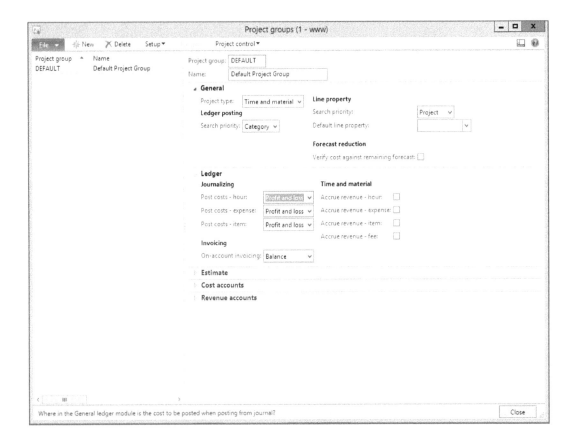

Set the **Project Group** to **DEFAULT** an the **Name** to **Default Project Group**. Set the **Project Type** to **Time and Material** if it is not already configured that way.

Configure Project Groups

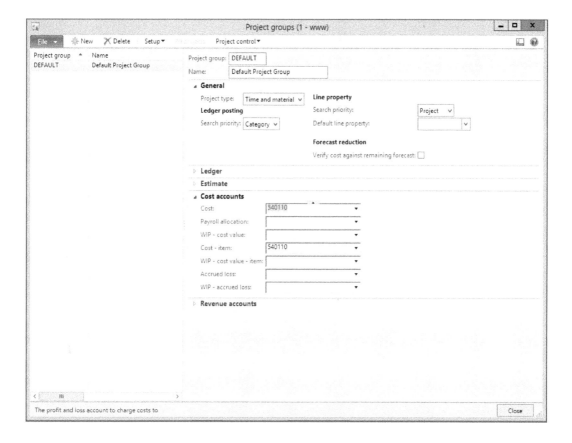

Expand the **Cost Accruals** tab, and configure any of the default accounts that you may need.

Configure Project Groups

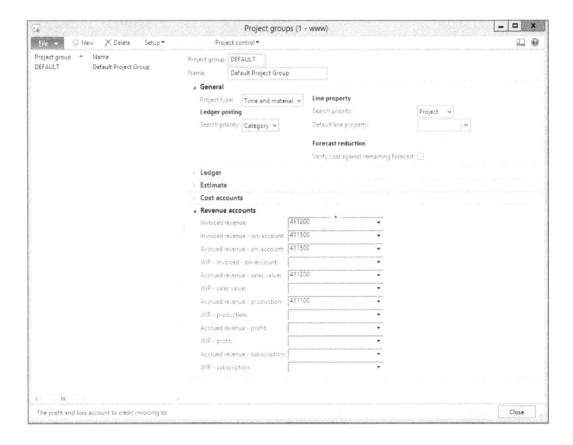

Then expand the **Revenue Accounts** tab and configure the key accounts there as well.

Configure Project Groups

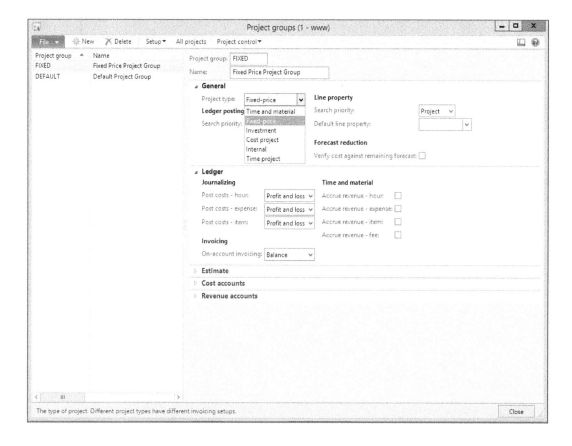

Click on the **New** button again, and create a new **Project Group** for fixed price projects. Set the **Project Group** to **FIXED**, and the **Name** to **Fixed Price Project Group**. From the **Project Type** dropdown box, select the **Fixed Price** option.

Configure Project Groups

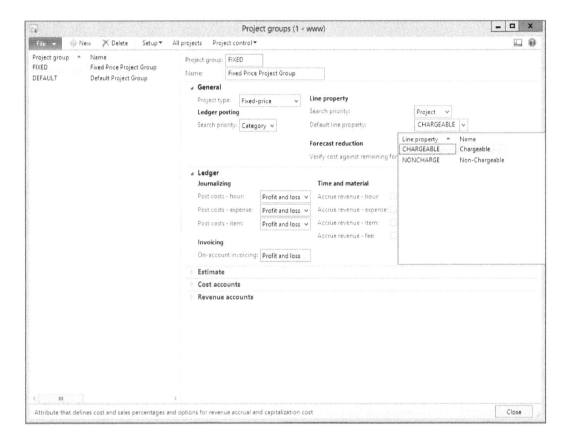

Also, for this one we will set the **Default Property Type** to **CHARGEABLE**.

Configure Project Groups

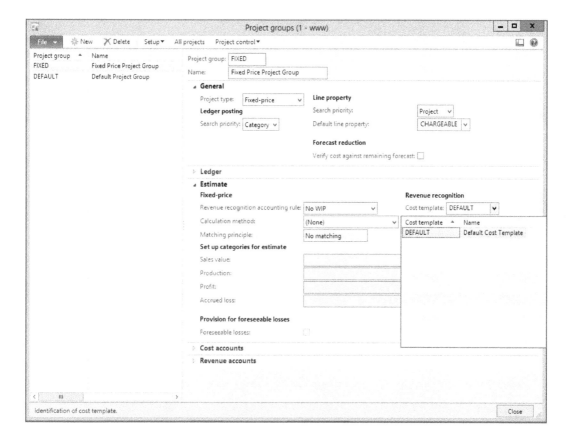

For the Fixed price project groups, we also need to expand the **Estimates** tab, and set the **Cost Template** to a value, In our case we set it to **DEFAULT**

Configure Project Groups

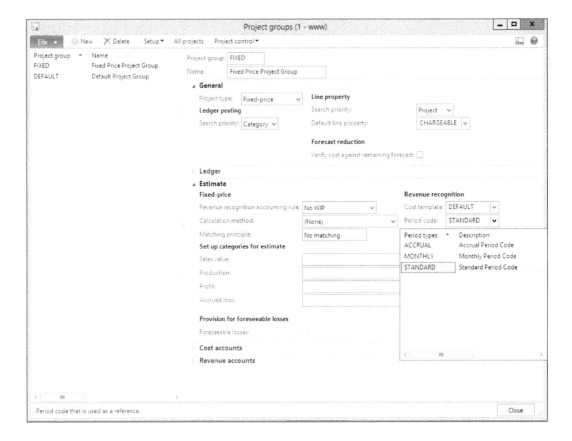

And then set the **Period Code** to **STANDARD**.

Configure Project Groups

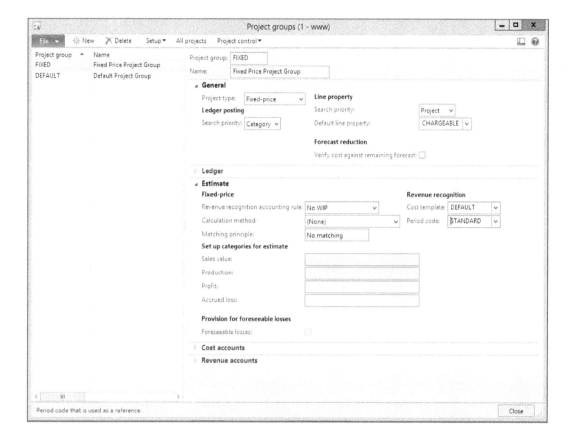

After you have done that, expand the **Cost Accounts**, and the **Revenue Accounts** tab and configure your default accounts the same way as in the previous record.

Then configure the default **Cost Accounts** and **Revenue Accounts** as you did with the first example.

After you have finished, click on the **Close** button to exit from the form.

Configuring Service Level Agreements

Now we will configure some example **Service Level Agreements**. These will be used on our **Service Agreements** to indicate our agreed upon response times.

Configuring Service Level Agreements

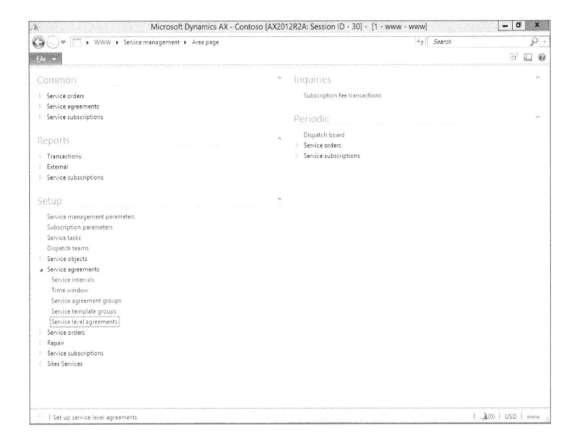

Click on the **Service Level Agreements** menu item within the **Service Agreements** folder of the **Setup** group within the **Service Management** area page.

Configuring Service Level Agreements

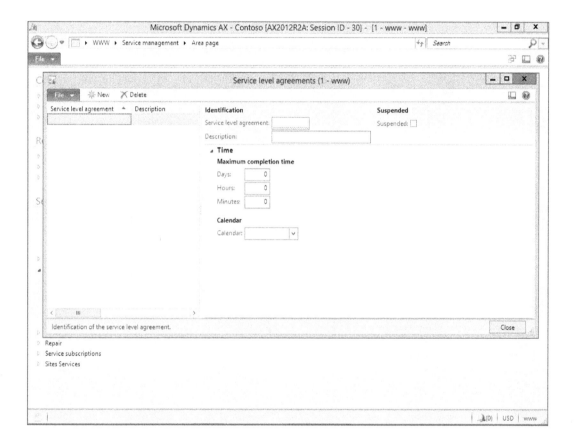

When the **Service Level Agreements** maintenance form is displayed, click on the **New** button to create a new record.

Configuring Service Level Agreements

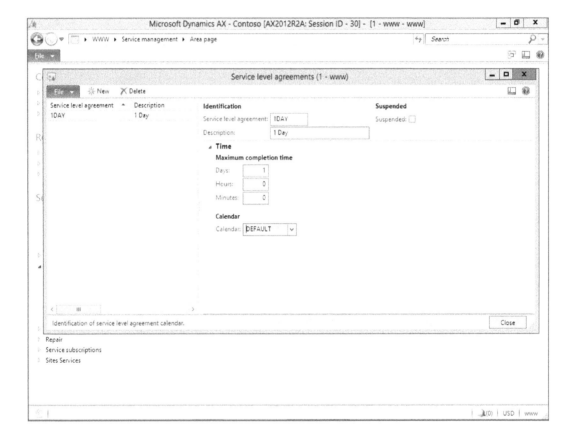

Give your record a **Service Level Agreement** code, and also a **Description**, and then set the time frame for the SLA.

Also, make sure that you set a default **Calendar** for your **Service Level Agreement.**

Configuring Service Level Agreements

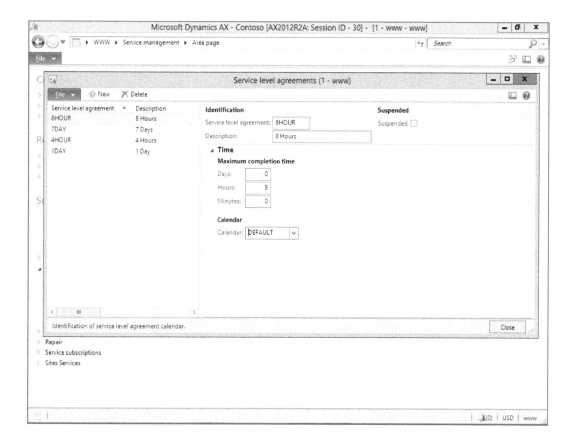

Continue adding as many other **Service Level Agreement** records, and when you are done, just click on the **Close** button to exit from the form.

Configure Service Agreement Groups

Now we will want to create a set of **Service Agreement Groups**. These will be used to segregate out **Service Agreements** later on into different groupings for reporting, and can also be used as a shorthand way to also specify different **Service Level Agreements** against **Service Agreements**.

Configure Service Agreement Groups

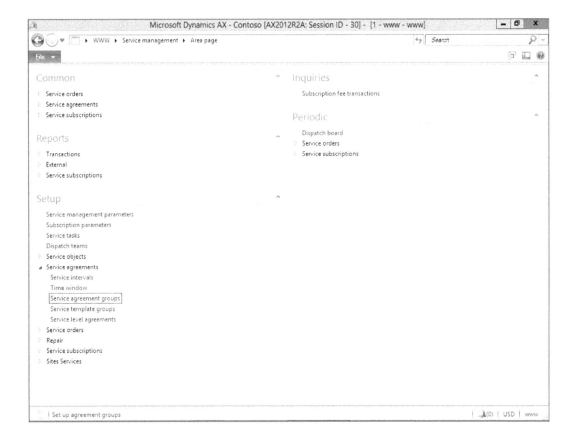

Click on the **Service Agreement Groups** menu item within the **Service Agreements** folder of the **Setup** group within the **Service Management** area page.

Configure Service Agreement Groups

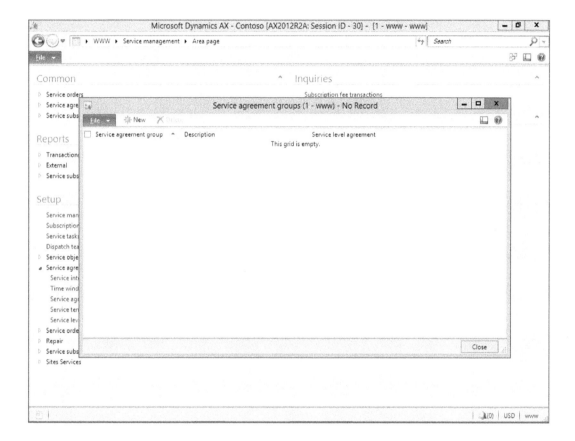

When the **Service Agreement Groups** maintenance form is displayed, click on the **New** button within the menu bar to

Configure Service Agreement Groups

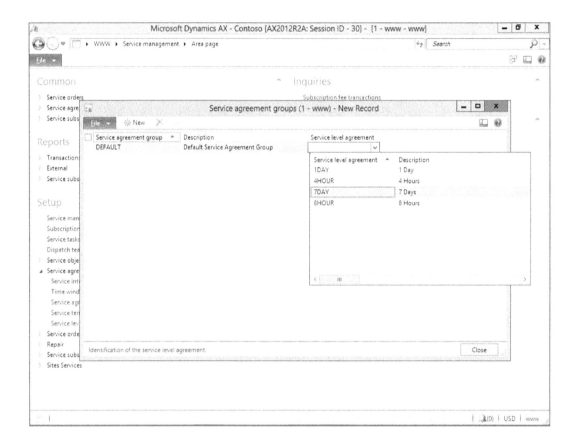

Configure Service Agreement Groups

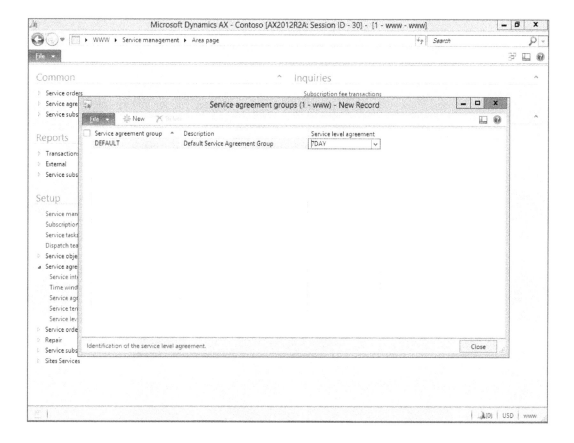

Configure Service Agreement Groups

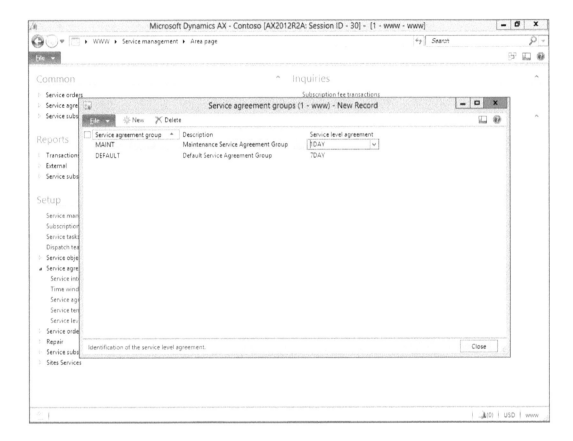

Continue creating **Service Agreement Groups** until you are done, and then click the **Close** button to exit the form.

Configure Service Management Journals

In order to perform many of the Service Management transactions, we need to configure a few **Journals** within Dynamics AX, but they are scattered around between the different areas, so in this section we will show you all of the **Journals** that you need.

Configure Service Management Journals

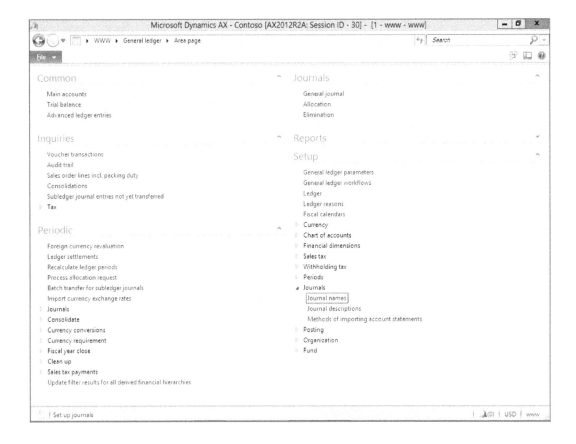

First we need to configure a **Project Expense Journal**. To do this, click on the **Journal Names** menu item within the **Journals** folder of the **Setup** group within the **General Ledger** area page.

Configure Service Management Journals

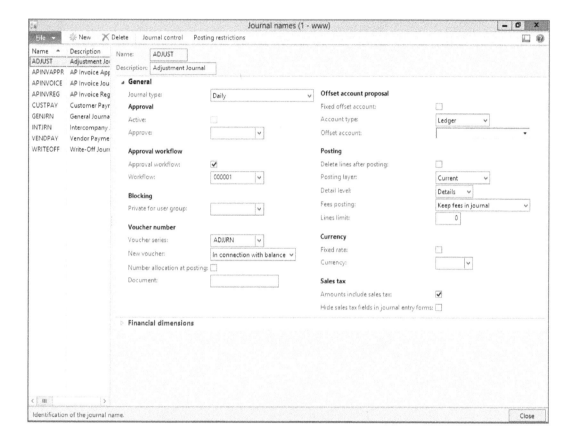

When the **Journal Names** maintenance form is displayed, click on the **New** button within the menu bar to create a new record.

Configure Service Management Journals

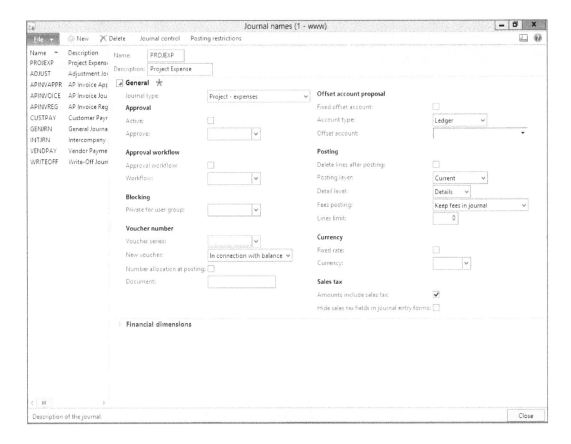

Set the **Name** to be **PROJEXP**, and the **Description** to **Project Expense**.

Configure Service Management Journals

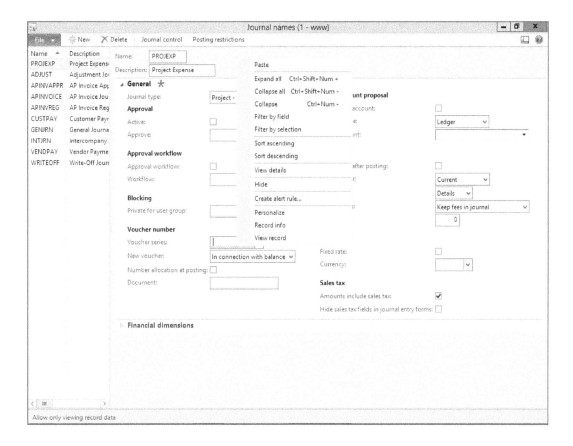

Now we need to create a new number sequence for our Journal. To do that, right-mouse-click on the **Voucher Series** field and click on the **View Details** menu item.

Configure Service Management Journals

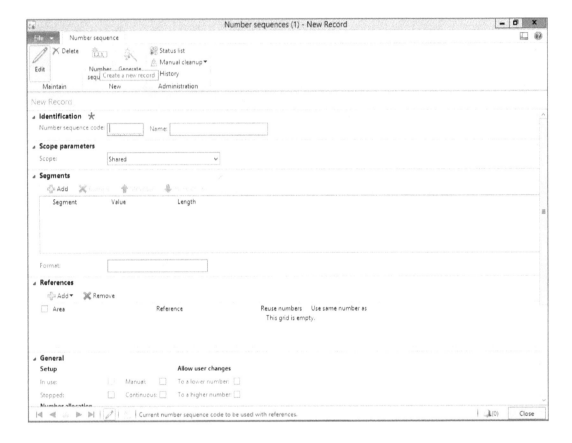

When the **Number Sequences** maintenance form is displayed, click on the **Number Sequence** button within the **New** group of the **Number Sequence** ribbon bar.

Configure Service Management Journals

Set the **Number Sequence Code** to **ProjExp_01** and the **Name** to **Project Expense**.

Then assign your number sequence a numbering format, and make sure you set the **Continuous** flag within the **General** tab.

When you are done, just click the **Close** button to exit from the form.

Configure Service Management Journals

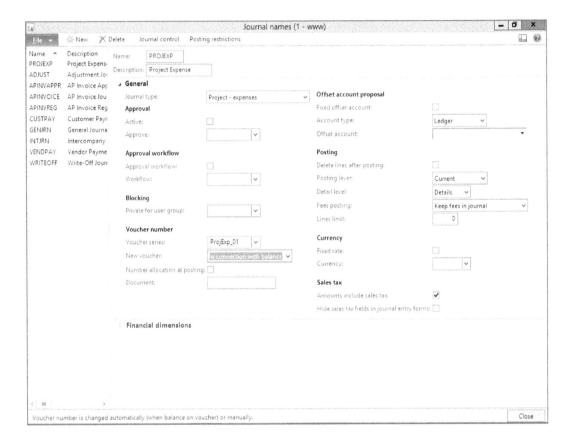

Now set the **Voucher Series** to be the new number sequence that you just created.

When you have done that, click the **Close** button to exit from the form.

Configure Service Management Journals

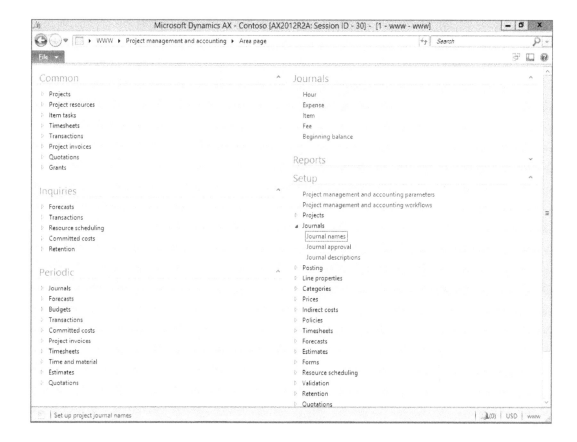

Now we need to set up a couple of journals for line level postings against the project for Expenses and Hours. To do that, click on the **Journal Names** menu item within the **Journals** folder of the **Setup** group within the **Project Management and Accounting** area page.

Configure Service Management Journals

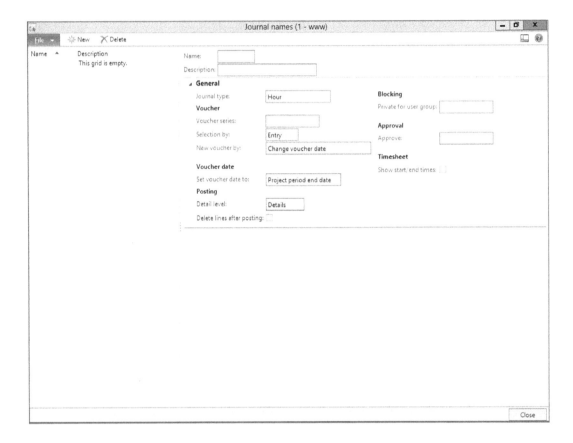

When the **Journal Names** maintenance form is displayed, click on the **New** button within the menu bar to create a new record.

Configure Service Management Journals

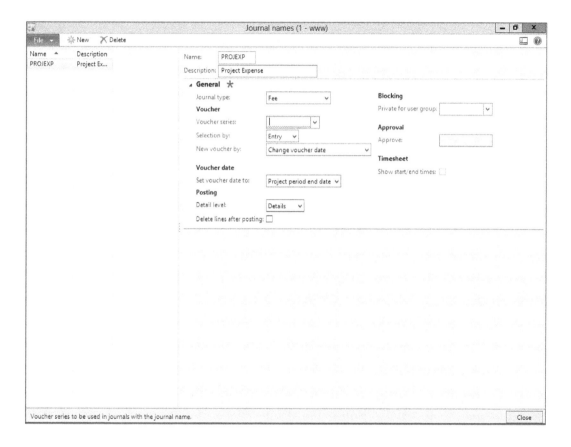

Set the **Name** to be **PROJEXP**, the **Description** to be **Project Expense** and make sure that the **Journal Type** is set to **Fee**.

Configure Service Management Journals

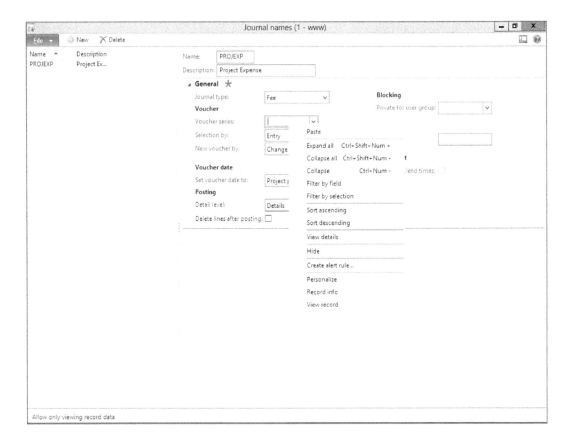

Then right-mouse-click on the **Voucher Series** field and select the **View Details** menu item.

Configure Service Management Journals

Set the **Number Sequence Code** to **ProjExp_02** and the **Name** to **Project Expense**.

Then assign your number sequence a numbering format, and make sure you set the **Continuous** flag within the **General** tab.

When you are done, just click the **Close** button to exit from the form.

Configure Service Management Journals

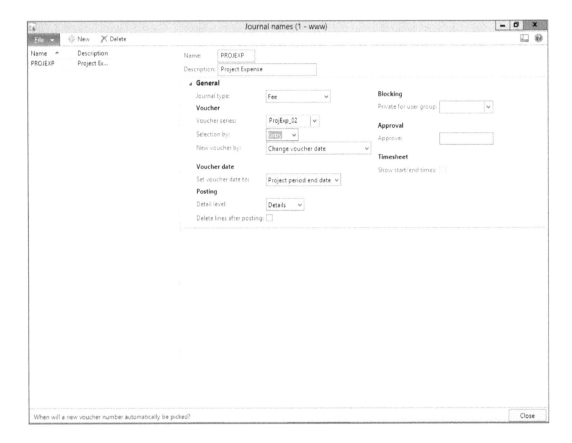

Now set the **Voucher Series** to be the new number sequence that you just created.

Then click on the **New** button within the menu bar to create a new record.

Configure Service Management Journals

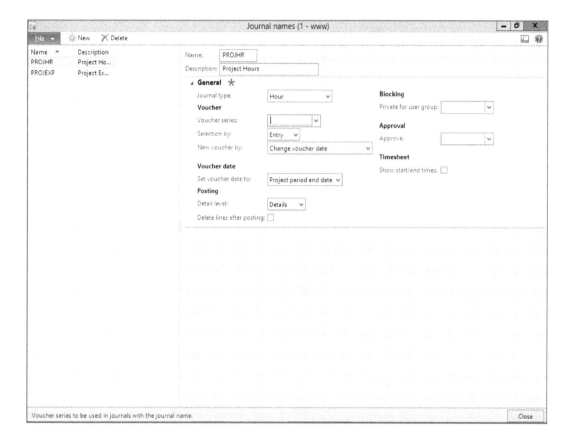

Set the **Name** to be **PROJHR**, the **Description** to be **Project Hours** and make sure that the **Journal Type** is set to **Hour**.

Configure Service Management Journals

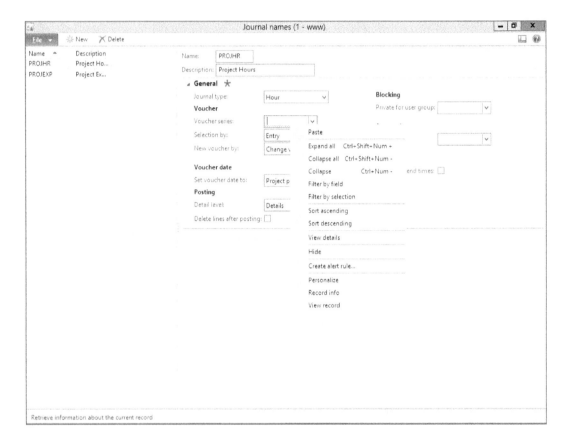

Then right-mouse-click on the **Voucher Series** field and select the **View Details** menu item.

Configure Service Management Journals

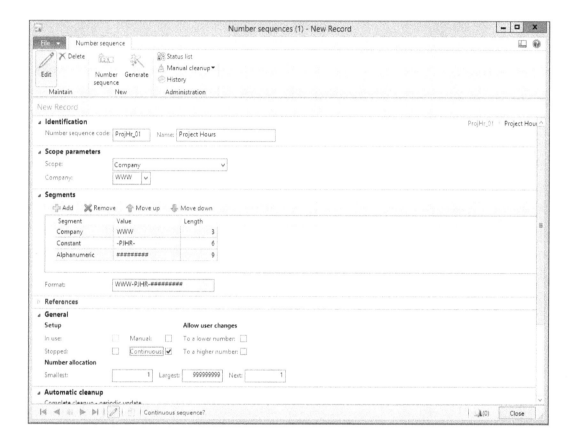

Set the **Number Sequence Code** to **ProjHr_01** and the **Name** to **Project Hours**.

Then assign your number sequence a numbering format, and make sure you set the **Continuous** flag within the **General** tab.

When you are done, just click the **Close** button to exit from the form.

Configure Service Management Journals

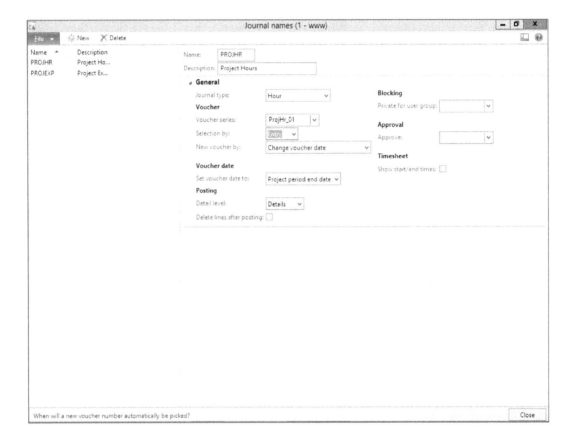

Now set the **Voucher Series** to be the new number sequence that you just created.

When you are done, click on the **Close** button to exit the form.

Configure Service Management Journals

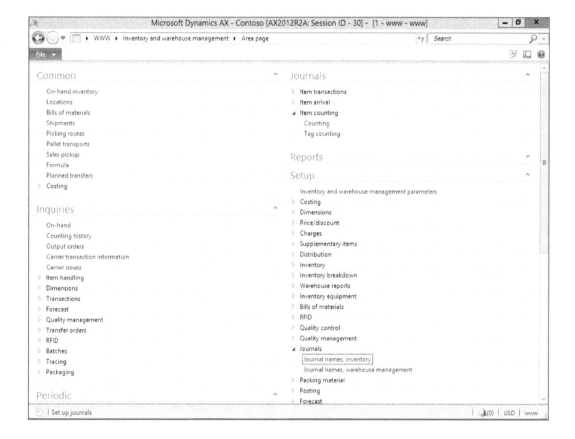

The final journal that we need to set up is within Inventory and is for the Project Item expenses. To do this, click on the **Journal Names, Inventory** menu item within the **Journals** folder of the **Setup** group within the **Inventory and Warehouse Management** area page.

Configure Service Management Journals

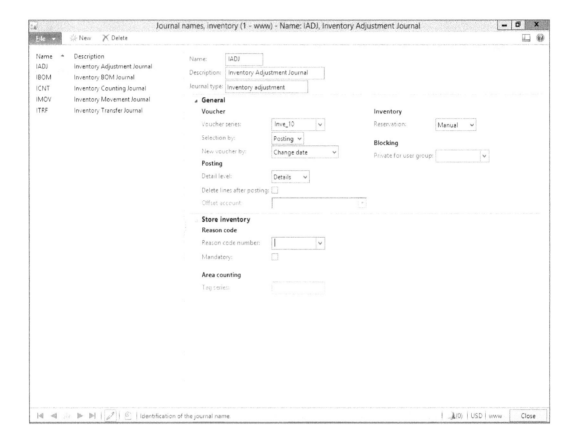

When the **Journal Names, Inventory** maintenance form is displayed, click the **New** button within the menu bar to create a new record.

Configure Service Management Journals

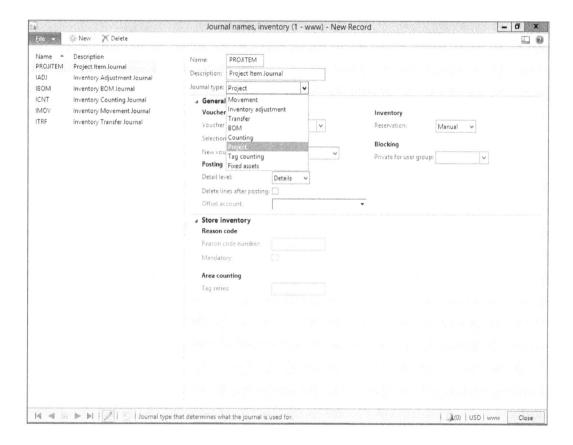

Set the **Name** to **PROJITEM**, the **Description** to **Project Item Journal** and then set the **Journal Type** to **Project**.

Configure Service Management Journals

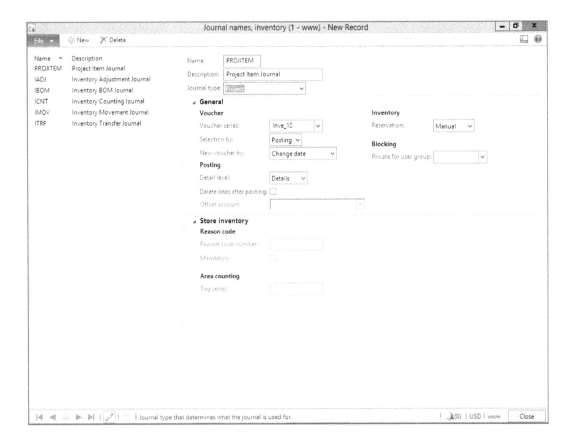

You don't have to create a new **Number Sequence** for this journal, so once you have done this, you can just click the **Close** button and exit from the form.

Configuring Service Order Stages

If you want to track the lifecycle of your **Service Orders** then you can easily do this through **Service Order Stages**. These allow you to define the stages that your Service Order will progress through, what transactions can be performed at any of the stages, and also when the Service Order is closed or not.

In this section we will show how you can configure your own **Service Order Stages**.

Configuring Service Order Stages

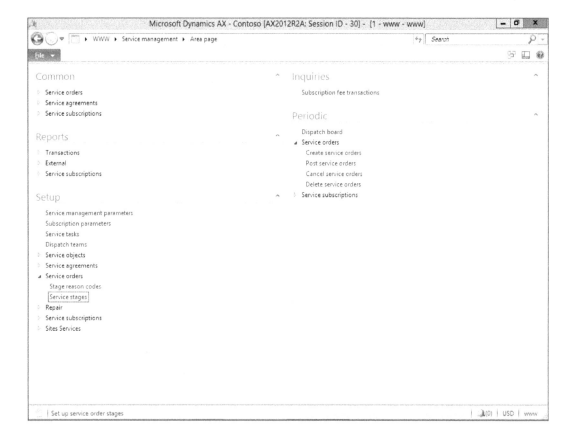

From the **Service management** area page, select the **Service stages** menu item from within the **Service orders** folder of the **Setup** group.

Configuring Service Order Stages

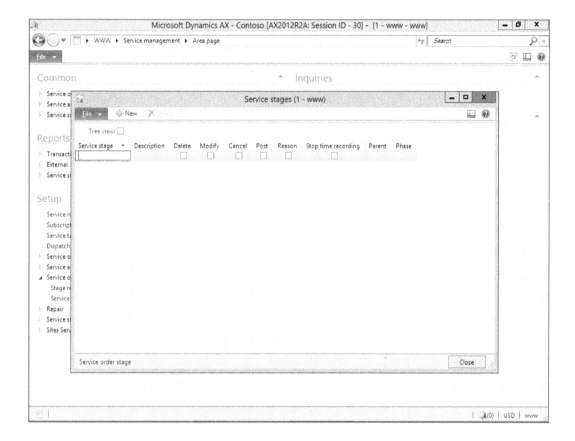

When the **Service stages** maintenance form is displayed, click on the **New** button in the menu bar to create the initial stage.

Configuring Service Order Stages

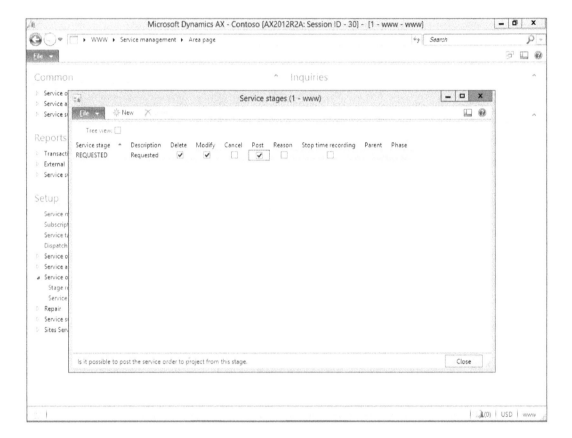

Give your stage a **Service stage** code, and a **Description**.

Then mark the valid operations that can be performed at the stage.

Note: You can use the **Service Stages** to manage when lines can be posted, if deletions are allowed and a lot more.

Configuring Service Order Stages

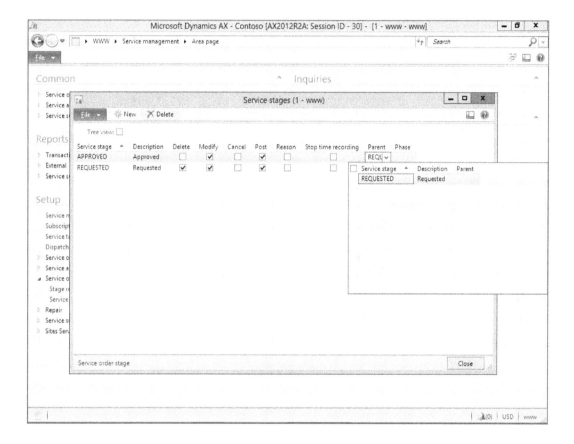

Add another **Service Stage**, but this time, make it a child of the first line by setting the **Parent** field to be the first entry.

Configuring Service Order Stages

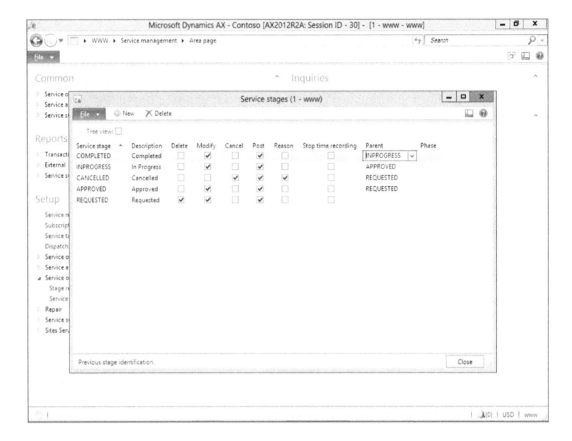

Continue adding additional stages to your **Service stages**, but for each additional stage, you will need to specify the parent **Service stage.**

Configuring Service Order Stages

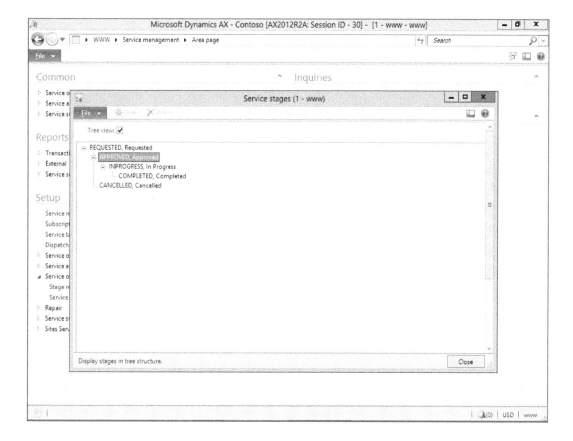

If you check the **Tree view** check box, then you will be able to see the complete route for the stages.

Configuring Service Reason Codes

If you mark any of the **Service Order Stages** to as having a **Reason** then you will also need to add a set of reason codes Dynamics AX for the **Service Stages** to reference.

In this example we will show how you can configure your own **Service Reason Codes**.

Configuring Service Order Stages

From the **Service management** area page, select the **Service reason codes** menu item from within the **Service orders** folder of the **Setup** group.

Configuring Service Order Stages

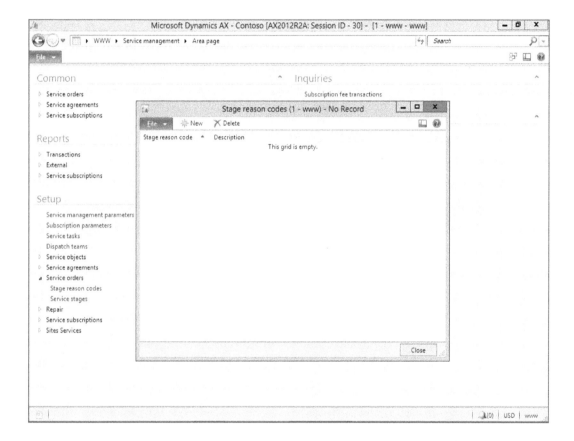

When the **Service reason code** maintenance form is displayed, click on the **New** button in the menu bar to create the initial stage.

Configuring Service Order Stages

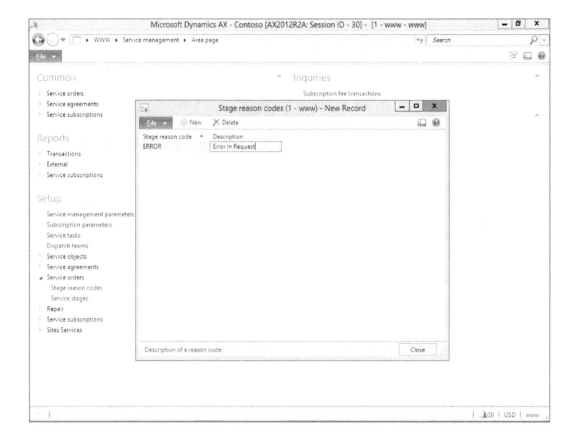

Give your stage a **Service reason code**, and a **Description**.

Configuring Service Order Stages

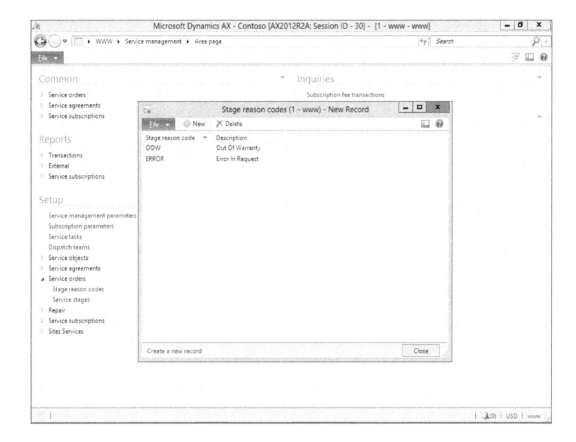

Continue adding additional reason codes, and when you are finished, click on the **Close** button to exit the form.

Creating Service Tasks

You can also define the tasks that you are allowed to perform against a **Service Agreement** as well through the **Service Tasks**.

In this section we will show how to configure **Service Tasks**.

Creating Service Tasks

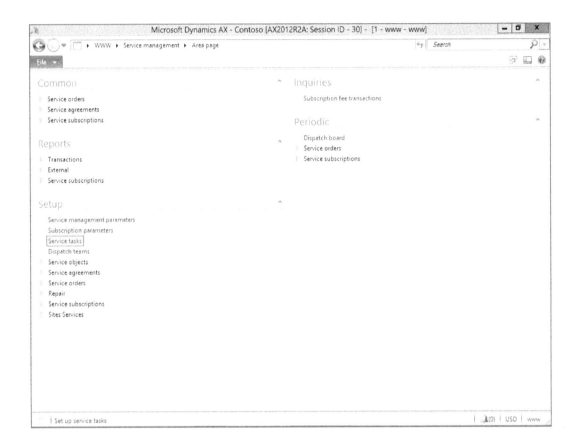

From the **Service management** area page, select the **Service tasks** menu item from the **Setup** group.

Creating Service Tasks

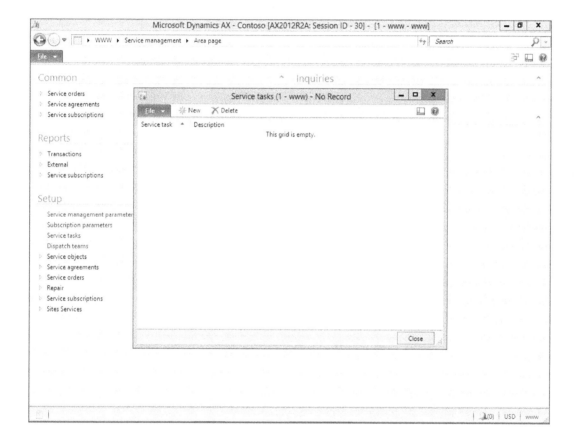

Within the **Service tasks** maintenance form, click the **New** button in the menu bar to create a **Service task** record.

Creating Service Tasks

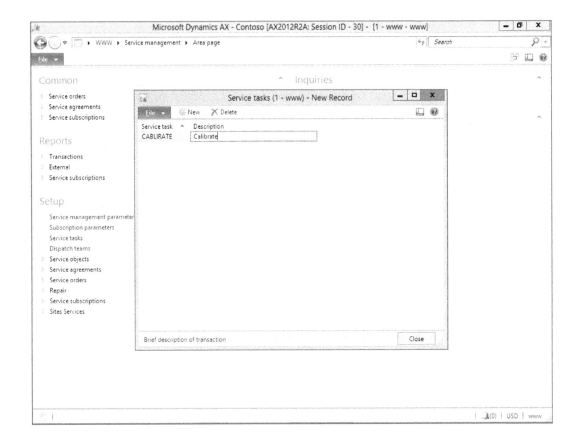

Then assign your **Service task** a code and **Description**.

Creating Service Tasks

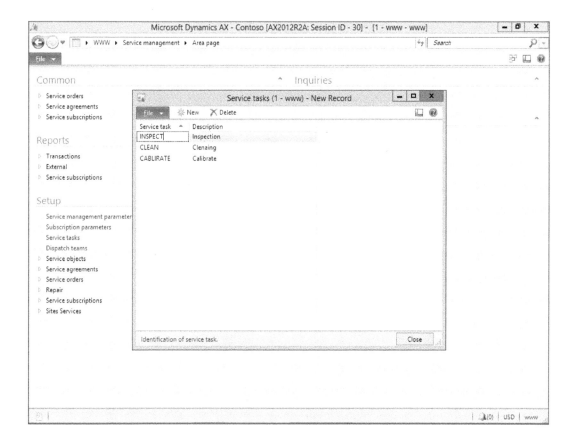

Repeat this process to add as many **Service Tasks** as you like and then click the **Close** button to exit the form.

Configuring Shared Categories

Now we will configure some **Shared Categories** that we can use within our **Project Cost Categories** which will manage all of our posting profiles.

Configuring Shared Categories

To do this click on the **Shared Categories** menu item in the **Categories** folder of the **Setup** group within the **Project Management and Accounting** area page.

Configuring Shared Categories

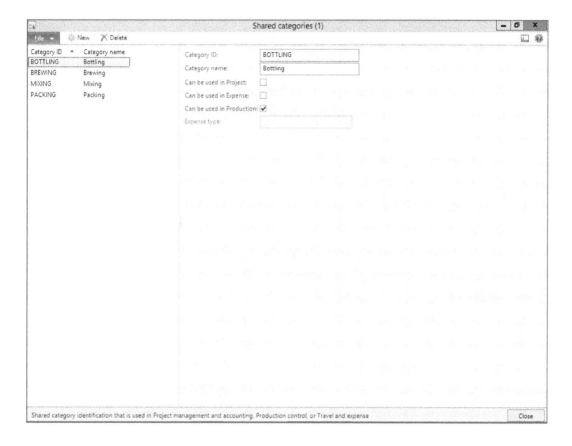

When the **Shared Categories** maintenance form is displayed, click on the **New** button within the menu bar to create a new record.

Configuring Shared Categories

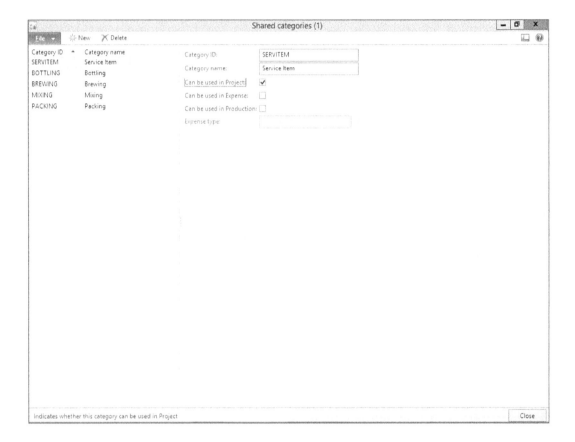

For this record, set the **Category ID** to be **SERVITEM**, the **Category Name** to **Service Item**, and make sure that the **Can Be Used In Project** flag is set.

Configuring Shared Categories

Repeat this process for **SERVLAB/Service Labor**, **SERVLABNC/Service Labor Non-Charge** and **SUBSCIP/Subscription Fee**.

After you have set up all of the Shared Categories, click the **Close** button to exit the form.

Configure Category Groups

Now we need to configure the **Category Groups** so that we can configure the default posting profiles for our **Project Categories**.

Configure Category Groups

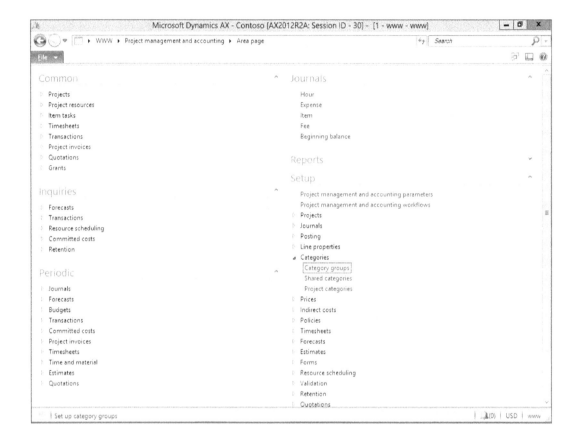

To do this, click on the **Category Groups** menu item within the **Categories** folder of the **Setup** group of the **Project Management and Accounting** area page.

Configure Category Groups

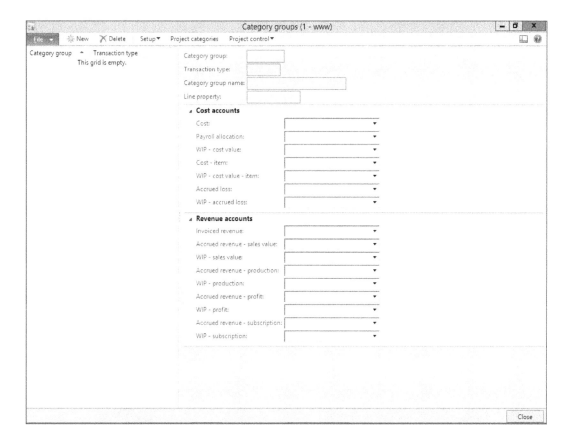

When the **Category Groups** maintenance form is displayed, click on the **New** button within the menu bar to create a new record.

Configure Category Groups

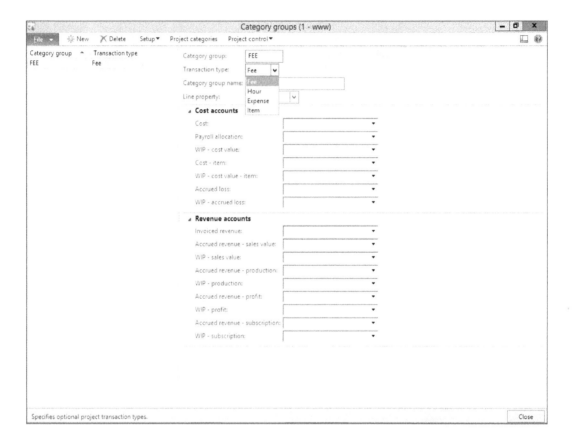

Set the **Category Group** to **FEE**, and select **Fee** from the **Transaction Type** dropdown.

Configure Category Groups

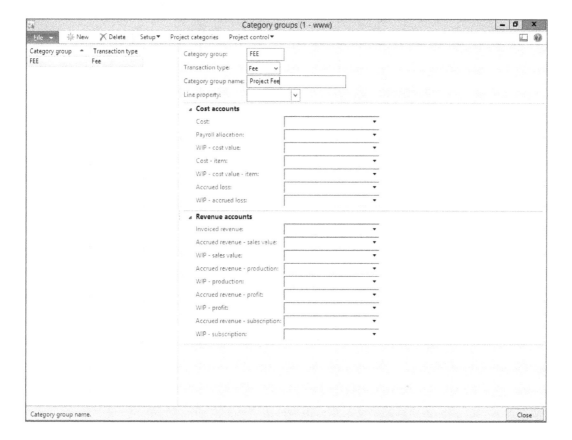

Finally, set the **Category Group Name** to **Project Fee.**

Configure Category Groups

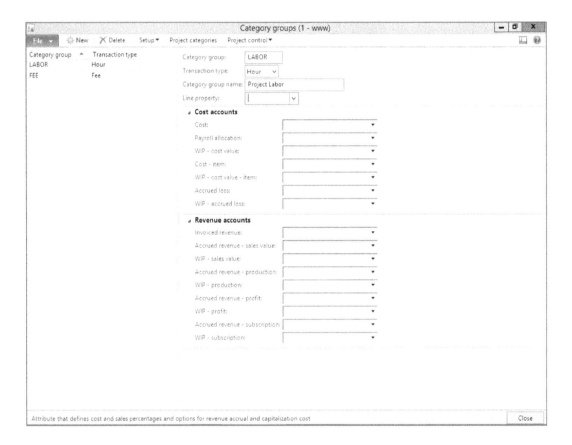

Create a new record, and set the **Category Group** to **LABOR**, the **Transaction Type** to **Hour**, and the **Category Group Name** to **Project Labor.**

Configure Category Groups

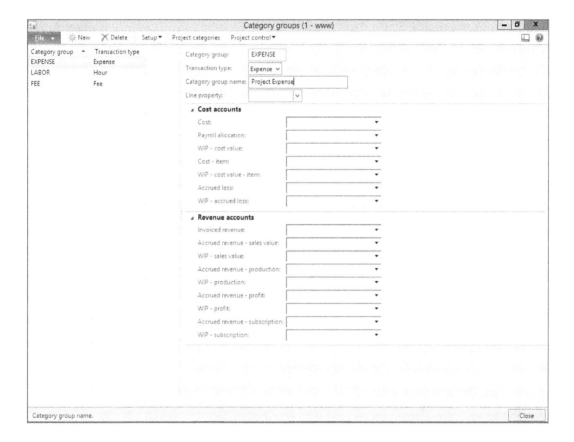

Create another new record, and set the **Category Group** to **EXPENSE**, the **Transaction Type** to **Expense**, and the **Category Group Name** to **Project Expense.**

Configure Category Groups

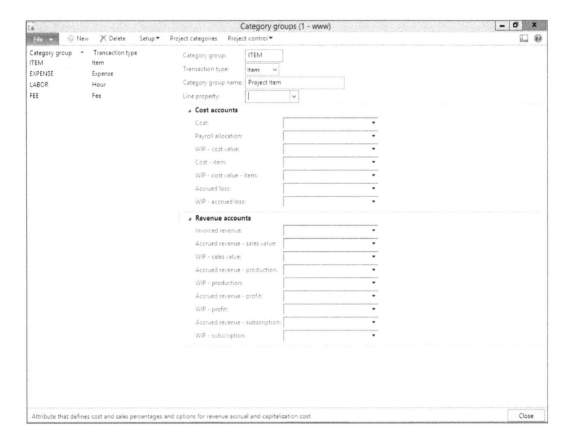

Create one last new record, and set the **Category Group** to **ITEM**, the **Transaction Type** to **Item**, and the **Category Group Name** to **Project Item.**

After you have done that just click on the **Close** button to exit the form.

Configuring Project Categories

The final codes that we need to configure are the **Project Categories** which will be used by **Service Management** to link the **Shared Categories**, and the **Category Groups**.

Configuring Project Categories

To do this, click on the **Project Categories** menu item within the **Categories** folder of the **Setup** group of the **Project Management and Accounting** area page.

Configuring Project Categories

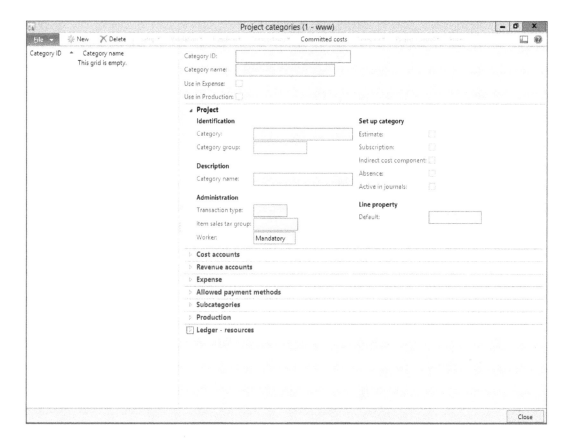

When the **Project Categories** maintenance form is displayed, click on the **New** button within the menu bar to create a new record.

Configuring Project Categories

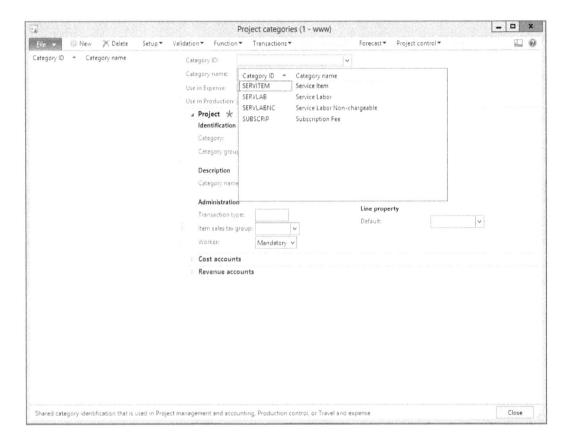

From the dropdown list for the **Category ID**, select the **SERVITEM** record.

Configuring Project Categories

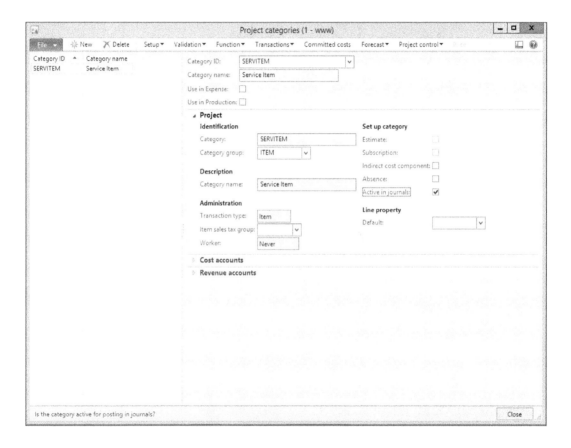

Then after the defaults are populated, check the **Active In Journal** flag within the **Project** tab.

Configuring Project Categories

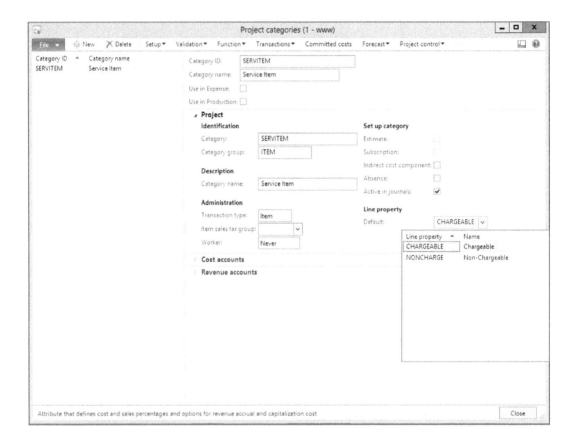

And then set the **Defaul** Line Property to **CHARGABLE**.

Configuring Project Categories

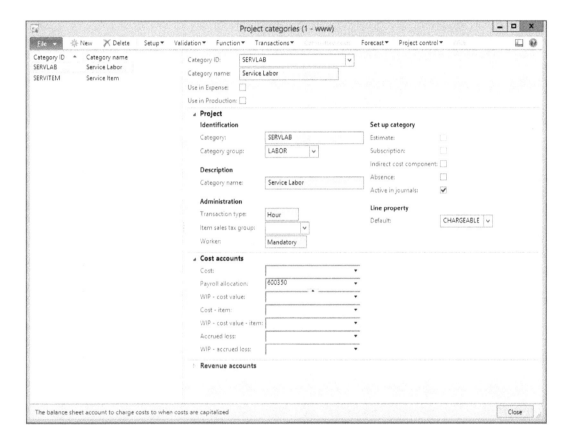

Repeat the process of adding a record, and set the **Category ID** to **SERVLAB**, making it **CHARGABLE**, and also **Active In Journals**.

Configuring Project Categories

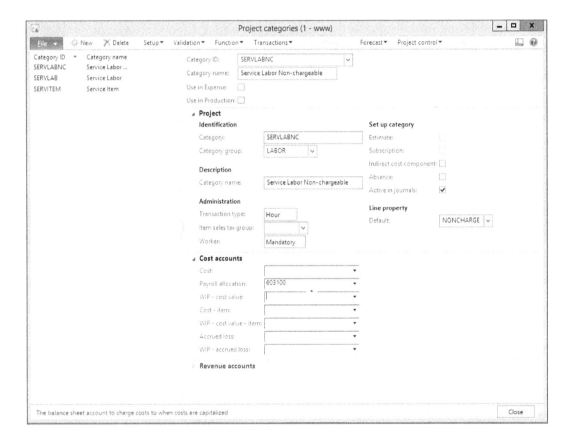

Repeat the process of adding a record, and set the **Category ID** to **SERVLABNC**, making it **NONCHARGE**, and also **Active In Journals**.

Configuring Project Categories

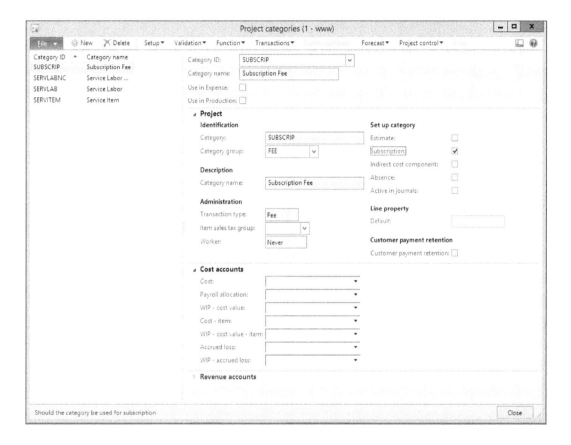

Repeat the process of adding a record one more time, and set the **Category ID** to **SUBSCRIP.** In this case check the Subscription flag within the **Set up Category** group.

Configuring Project Categories

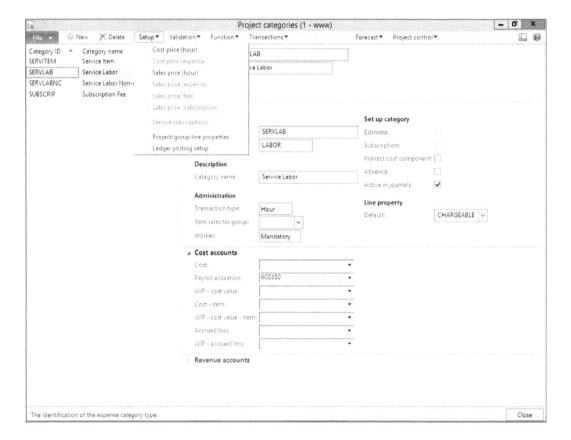

Also, if you want to update the default costs for the labor that is being assigned to the **Service Order** then select the **Cost price** menu item from the **Setup** menu item.

Configuring Project Categories

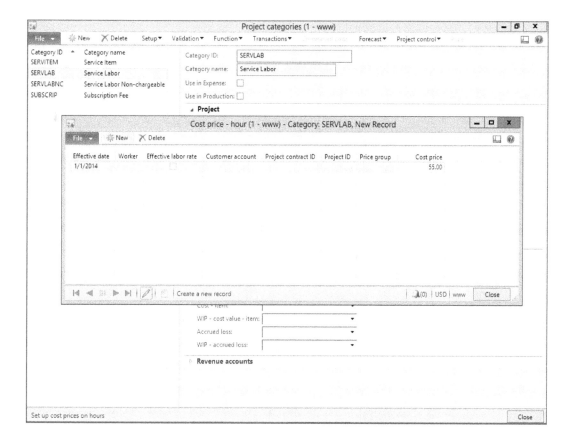

This will allow you to specify the default rates that will be applied when these **Project categories** are used on a **Service Order**. To set a default cost against the Labor, just click on the **New** button within the menu bar and set the cost with an effective date.

Configuring Project Categories

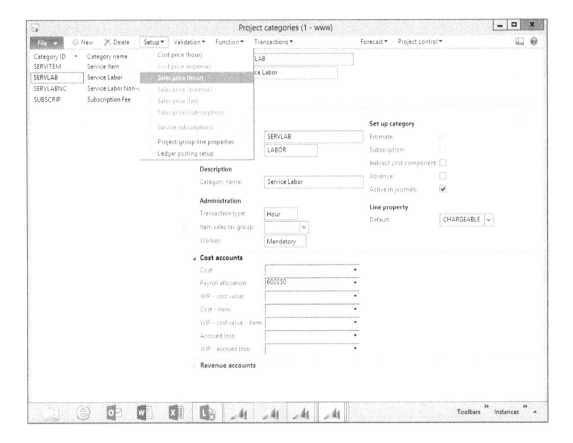

If you want to update the default prices for the labor that is being assigned to the **Service Order** then select wither the **Cost price** or **Sales price** options from the **Setup** menu item.

Configuring Project Categories

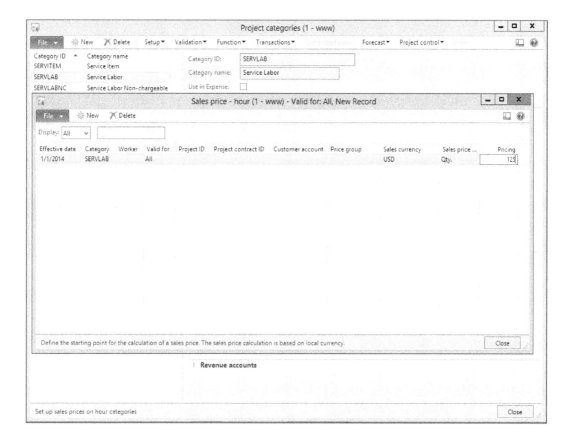

This will allow you to specify the default prices that will be applied when these **Project categories** are used on a **Service Order**. To set a default price against the Labor, just click on the **New** button within the menu bar and set the cost with an effective date.

When you are finished, you can just close out of the forms by clicking on the **Close** button.

Configure Service Management Parameters

Now that we have all of the main codes and controls configured for **Service Management** the final task is just to configure the **Service Management** parameters to make sure that everything is going to work the way that we expect it to.

Configure Service Management Parameters

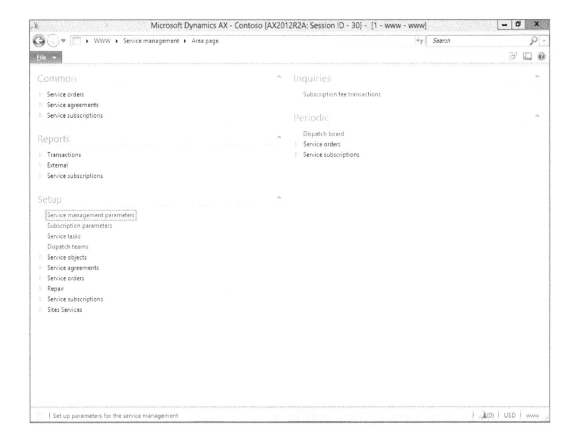

To do this, click on the **Service Management Properties** menu item within the **Setup** group of the **Service Management** area page.

Configure Service Management Parameters

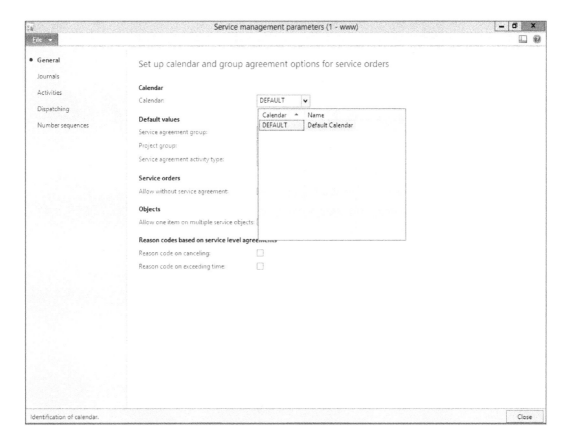

When the **Service Management Parameters** form is displayed, start on the **General** tab, and set the **Calendar** to your default working calendar.

Configure Service Management Parameters

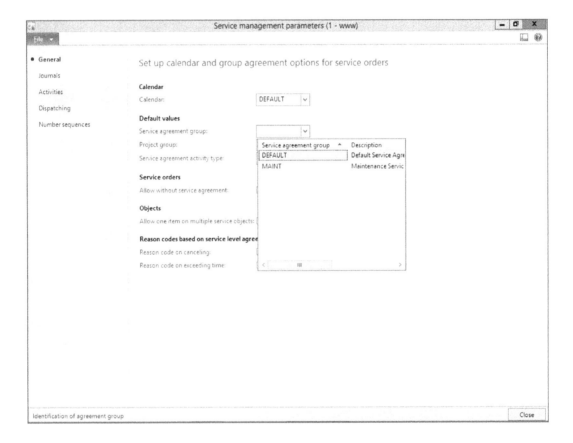

Set the default **Service Agreement Group**.

Configure Service Management Parameters

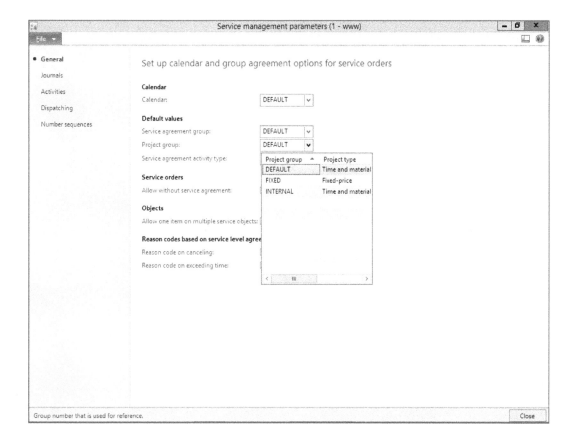

Set the default **Project Group**.

Configure Service Management Parameters

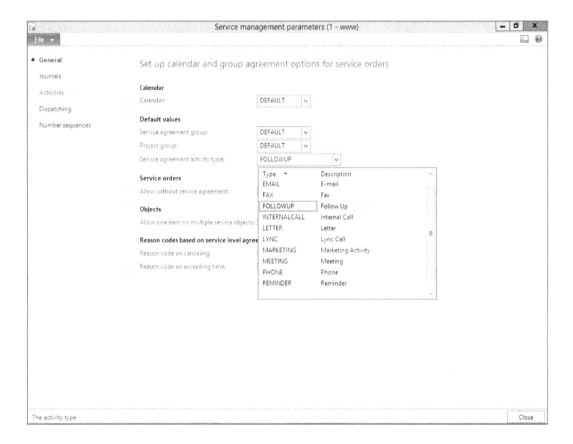

Then set the **Service Agreement Activity Type** that will be used when creating activities for the dispatch team.

Configure Service Management Parameters

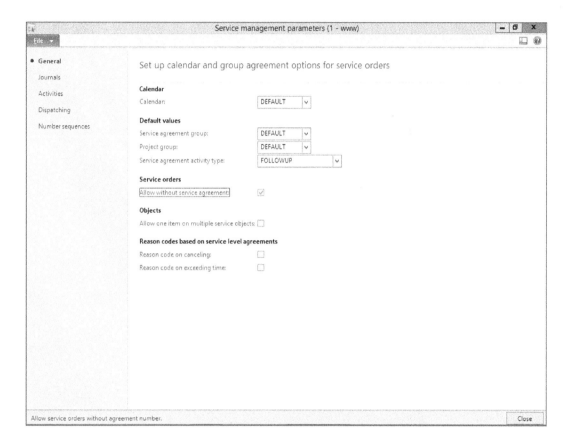

Finally, you may also want to set the **Allow without service agreement** checkbox. This will allow you to create Service Orders on the fly even when you don't have a Service Agreement established with the customer.

Configure Service Management Parameters

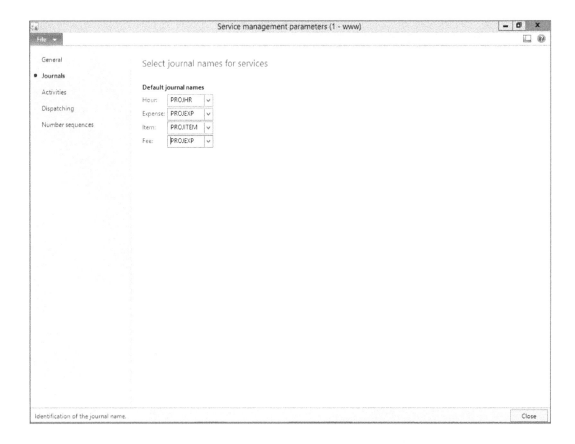

Now switch to the **Journals** tab, and set the **Default Journal Names** to be the new project journals that you just created.

Configure Service Management Parameters

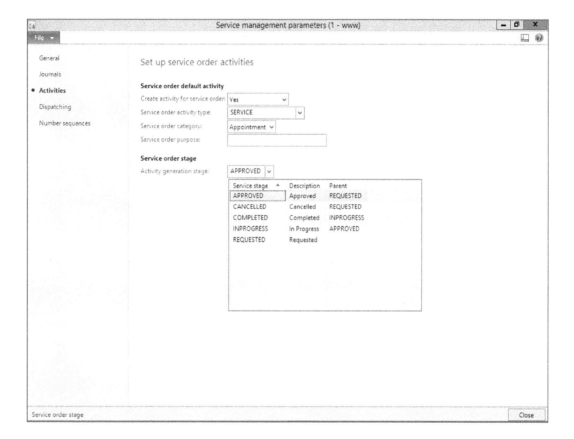

Now switch to the **Activities** tab. Set the **Activity Generation Stage** to be one of the **Service Stages** that you configured. This is a very important step, because if you do not set this value, then the service orders will not create activities for the dispatch team, and your dispatch board will never have any data.

Configure Service Management Parameters

The final step is to switch to the **Dispatching** tab, and define the default **Days Before** and **Days After** that will be used by the **Dispatch Board**. When you open up the dispatch board, it will calculate the date range that will be shown based on these defaults. Don't set them too small, otherwise the default window will be too small, and don't set them too large, otherwise you will be forever searching for service orders.

Also, you can set the color coding for the service orders.

When you are finished, just click the **Close** button to exit the form.

SERVICE ORDERS

Now that we have all of the codes and controls configured within Dynamics AX, we can start creating transactions, and the best place to start is with the **Service Orders**.

In this section we will show how the **Service Orders** are managed, and how you can use them by themselves to track your jobs.

Creating A Service Order Project

Before we start creating service orders though, there is one small task that we need to perform. Although we have all of the codes and controls configured for **Service Management** and **Project Accounting** we haven't created a base **Project** that we will use to track all of the costs and transactions for the **Service Orders** against.

In this section we will show you how to quickly create a generic **Project** that we will be able to use with our **Service Orders.**

Creating A Service Order Project

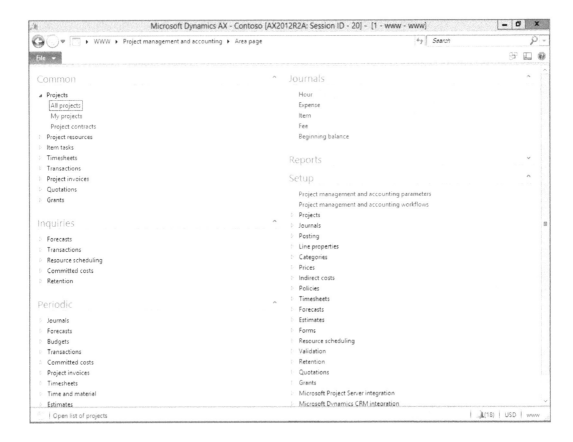

Click on the **All Projects** menu item within the **Projects** folder of the **Common** group of the **Project Management and Accounting** area page.

Creating A Service Order Project

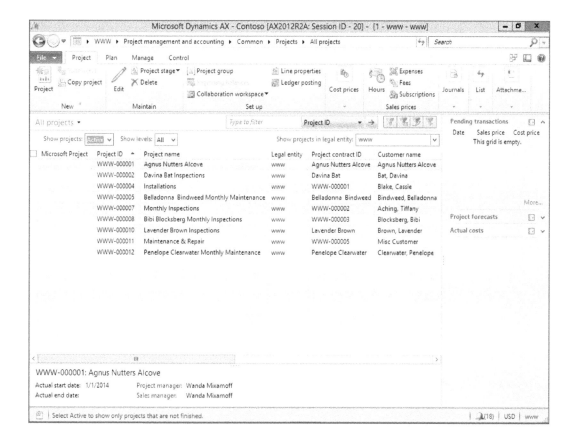

When the **All Projects** list page is displayed, click on the **Project** button within the **All** group of the **Projects** ribbon bar.

Creating A Service Order Project

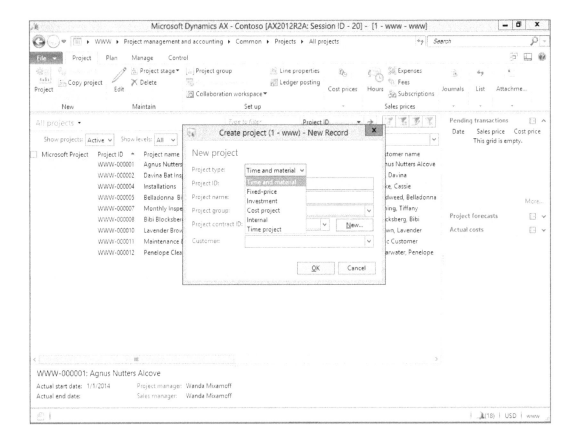

When the **Create Project** dialog box is displayed, select the **Project Type** that you want to associate with the **Project**.

Note: Make sure that you select one that has corresponding **Project Groups** from the previous sections setup.

Creating A Service Order Project

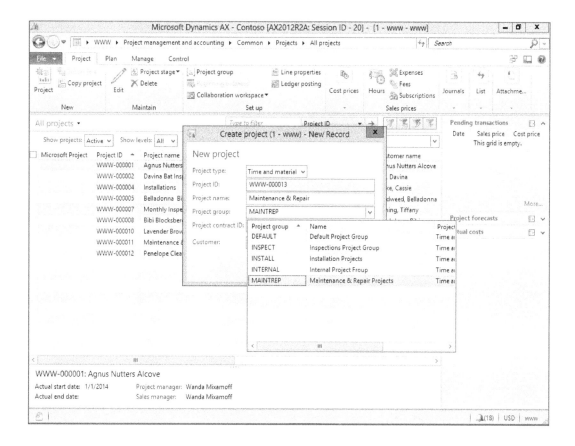

Give your **Project** a **Project Name**, and then select a **Project Group** that you want to associate the **Project** with.

Creating A Service Order Project

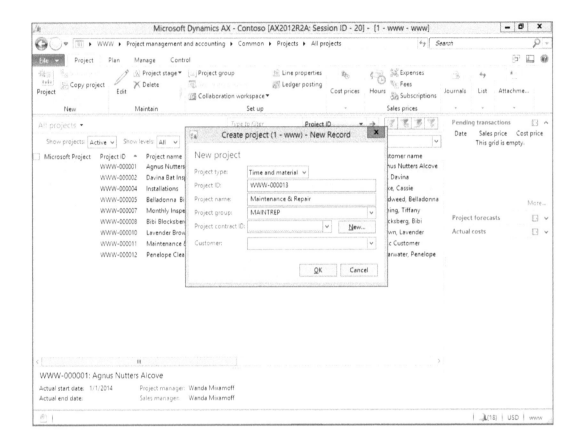

Next, if you don't have any **Project Contracts** configured, create one by clicking on the **New** button to the right of the **Project Contract Group** field.

Creating A Service Order Project

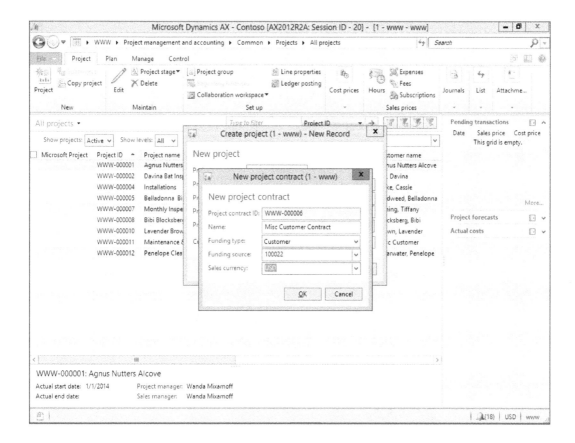

When the **New Project Contract** dialog box is displayed, give your **Project Contract** a **Name**, select a **Funding Type**, and **Funding Source**, and then click on the **OK** button to create the record.

Creating A Service Order Project

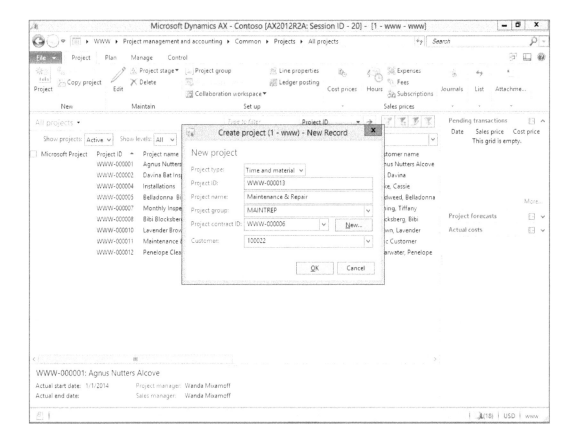

When you return to the **create Project** dialog box, the **Project Contract ID**, and **Customer** should already be filled in for you and you can click the **OK** button to create your **Project**.

Creating A Service Order Project

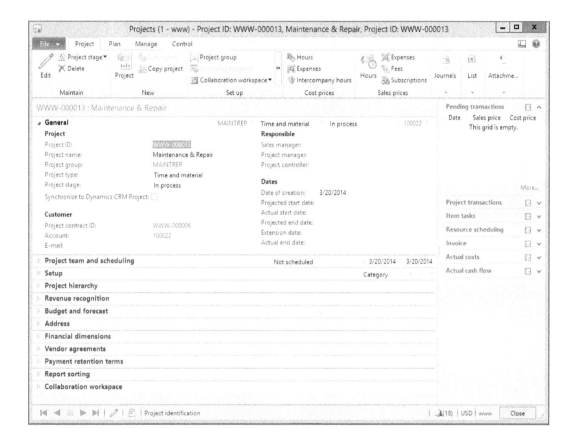

When the **Projects** maintenance form is displayed, just click the **Close** button to exit from the form.

Creating a Service Order

Now we can start creating a **Service Order**. Although we can automate this task later on through the **Service Agreements**, if you want to create ad-hoc **Service Orders** then that's an easy task.

Creating A Service Order

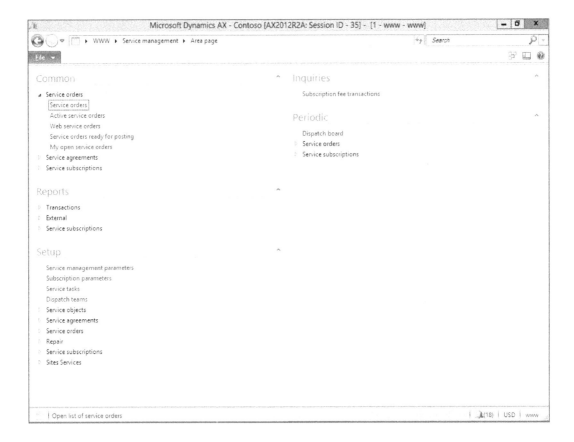

To do this, just click on the **Service Orders** menu button within the **Service Orders** folder of the **Common** Group within the **Service Management** area page.

Creating A Service Order

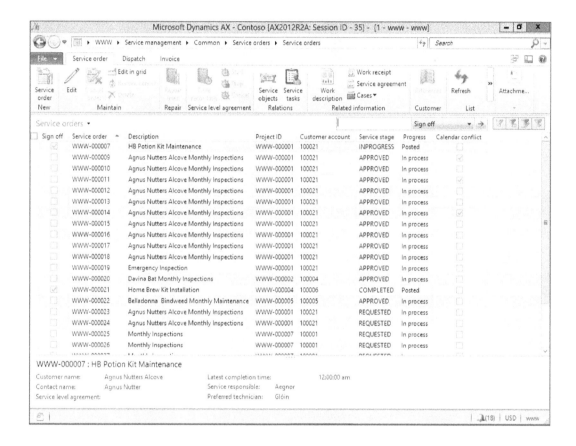

When the **Service Orders** list page is displayed, just click on the **Service Order** button within the **New** group of the **Service Order** ribbon bar.

Creating A Service Order

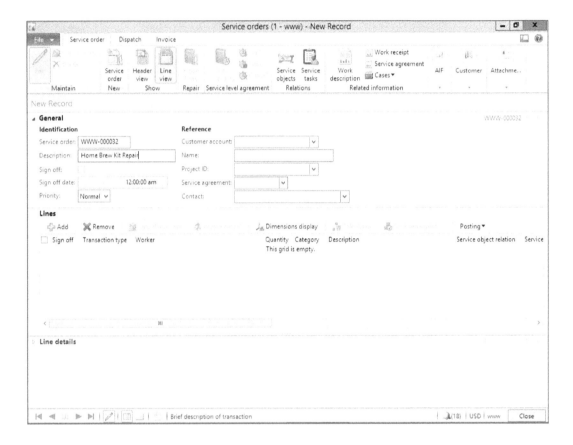

When the **Service Order** maintenance form is displayed, add a **Description.**

Creating A Service Order

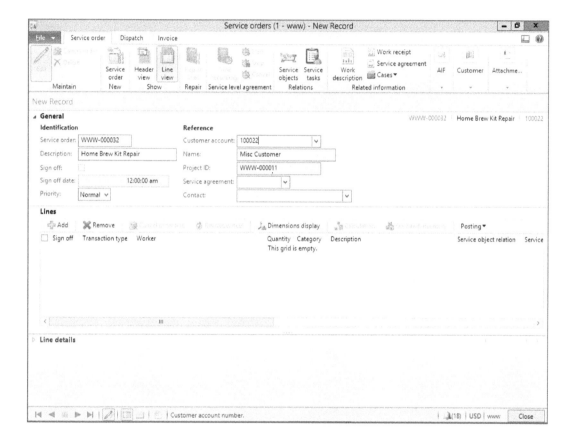

Then select the **Project ID** that you want to use to track the **Service Order** through. This will automatically default in a **Customer Account,** but you have the option to override this at this point if you are using a common **Project** to track multiple accounts service orders.

You are now done, and you can click the **Close** button to exit from the form.

Updating Service Order Stages

Now that you have a **Service** Order, you can start tracking the progress of it through the **Service Stages** that you configured in the first section.

Updating Service Order Stages

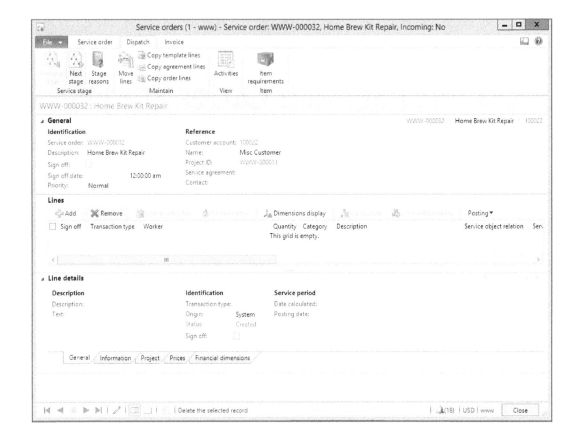

To change the state of the **Service Order**, just select the record, and then click on the **Next Stage** button within the **Service stage** group of the **Dispatch** ribbon bar.

Updating Service Order Stages

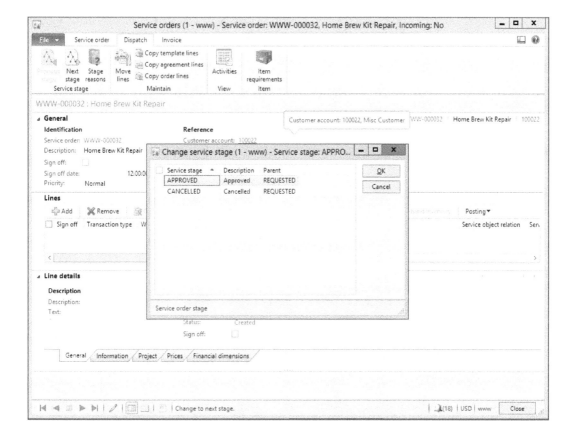

If you have defined multiple options for the next stage in the process, then you will be asked which stage you would like to move the **Service Order** into. Select the option, and then click the **OK** button.

Updating Service Order Stages

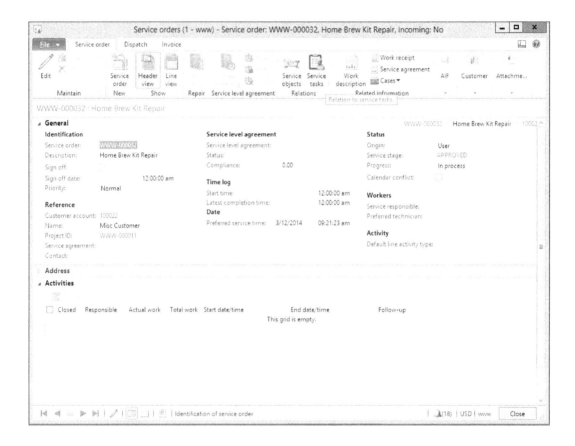

Now you will see that the **Service stage** for the **Service Order** has change the next stage in the process.

Printing Service Order Work Instructions

Once the **Service Orders** are created, you can also print the **Work Instructions**.

Printing Service Order Work Instructions

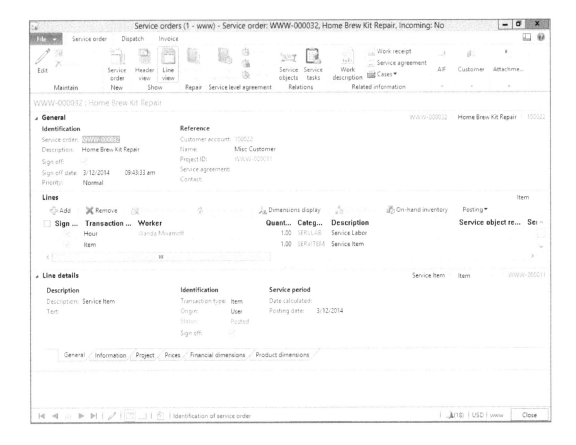

From your **Service Order** click on the **Work Description** button within the **Related Information** group of the **Service Orders** ribbon bar.

Printing Service Order Work Instructions

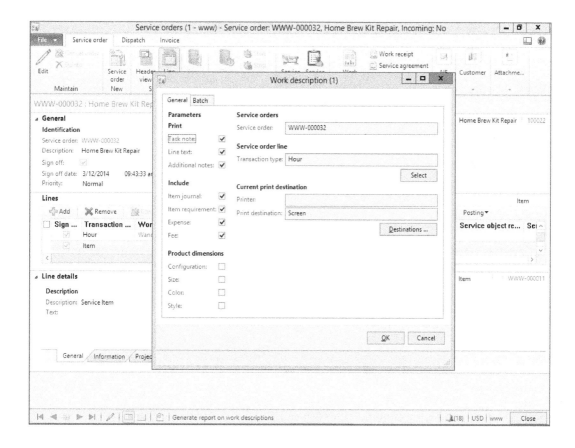

When the print dialog is displayed, select the options that you want to include in the **Work Instructions** and then click the **OK** button.

Printing Service Order Work Instructions

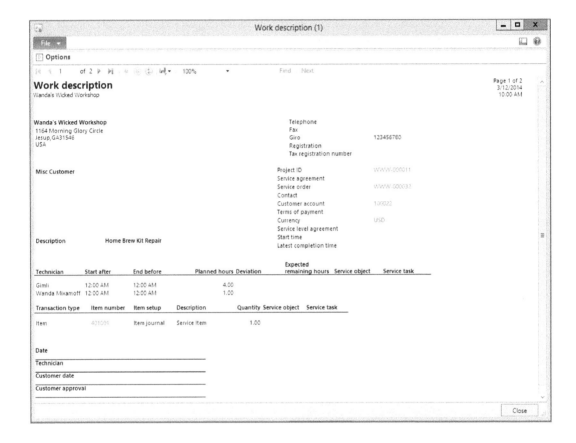

This will print out all of your work instructions for you technician to use and sign off on.

Posting Time To A Service Order

Once you have a **Service Order** that is in a **Service** Stage that allows for posting, you can start posting time and materials to it, and recording activity.

Posting Time To A Service Order

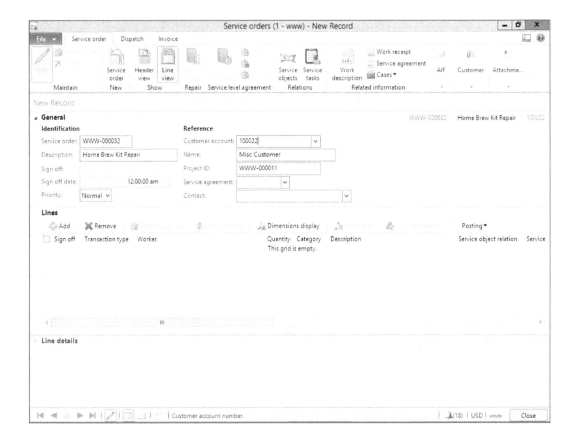

From within the **Lines** tab on the **Service order** click on the **Add** button in the tool bar to create a new service order line.

Posting Time To A Service Order

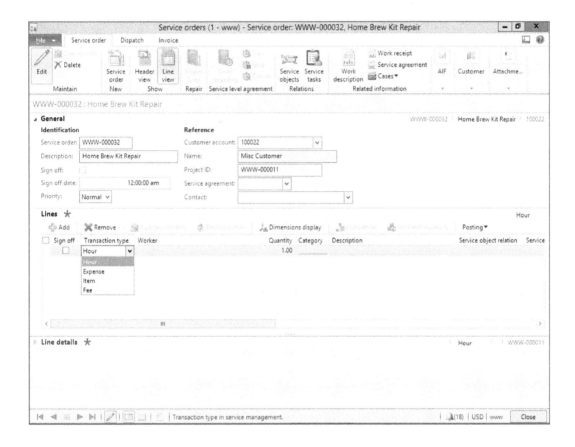

To post time against the **Service Order** select *Hour* from the **Transaction type** drop down.

Posting Time To A Service Order

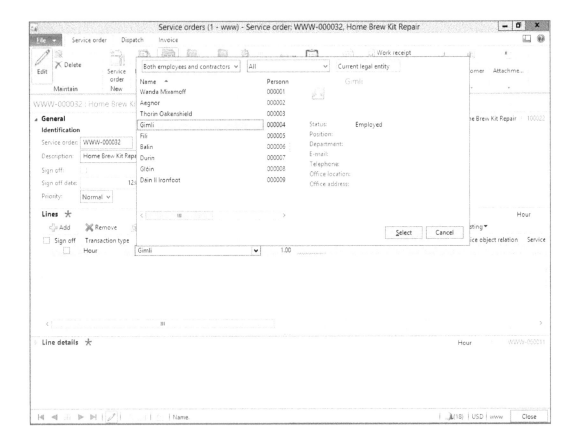

Now select the **Worker** that you are posting time for.

Posting Time To A Service Order

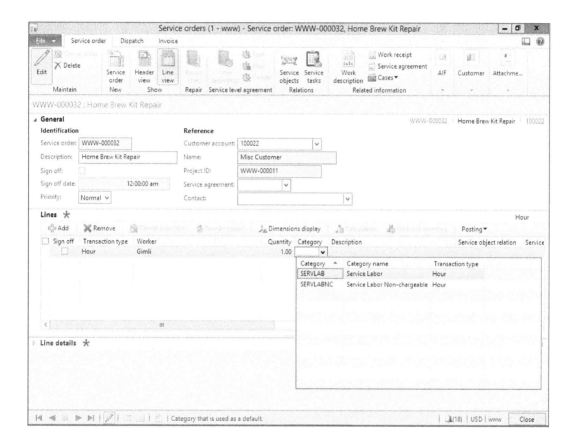

Select the **Category** for the line from the drop down to specify the type of labor that is being assigned to the **Service Order**.

Posting Time To A Service Order

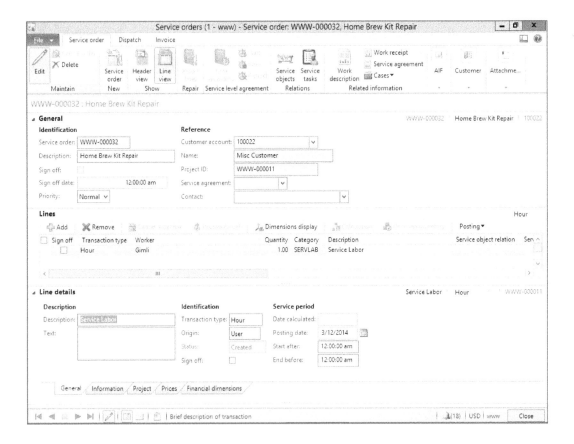

If you open up the **Line Details** tab, and select the **General** tab, then you will notice that you can change the **Description**, and also add more details within the **Text** field.

Posting Time To A Service Order

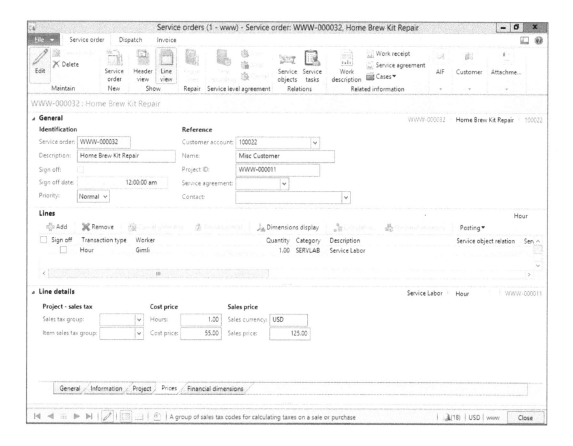

Also, if you select the **Prices** tab within the **Line Details** then you will be able to adjust the price that has defaulted in from the **Category** that we configured within the first section.

Posting Through The Service Management Portal

The Service Management area also has a web portal that allows you to view and update **Service Orders**, and **Agreements** through a web site.

Posting through the Service Management Portal

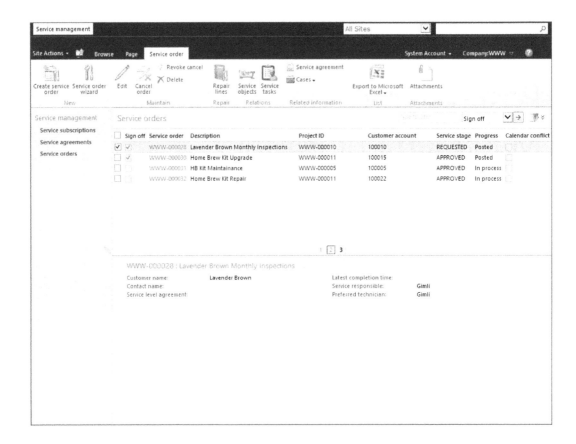

The **Service management portal** is part of the default Enterprise Portal. As soon as you access it, you will be able to see all of the same information that is available through the traditional windows client.

Posting through the Service Management Portal

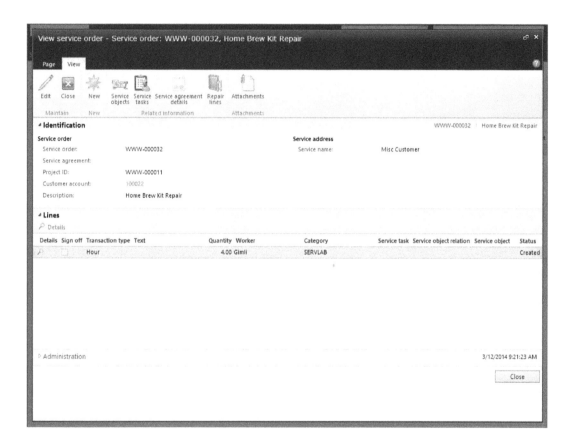

If you select the **Service Order** that you just entered, then you will be able to see all the same detail within the web client as you saw within the rich client.

Posting through the Service Management Portal

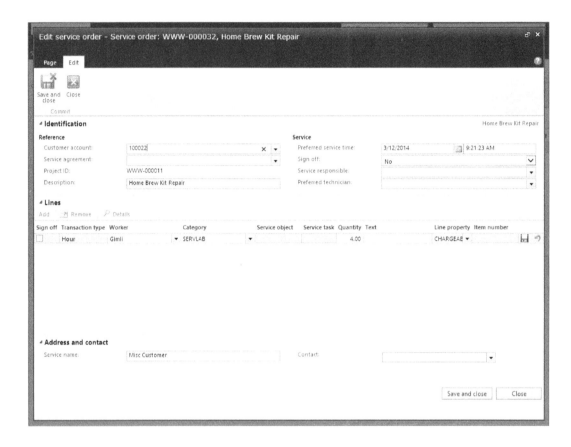

You can click on the edit pencil to the left of the lines, and update the information that you just added.

To post more time against the **Service Order** all you need to do is click on the **Add** button within the **Lines** menu bar.

Posting Through The Service Management Portal

This will step you through a wizard where you can select the **Transaction Type**, and then click the **Next** button.

Posting Through The Service Management Portal

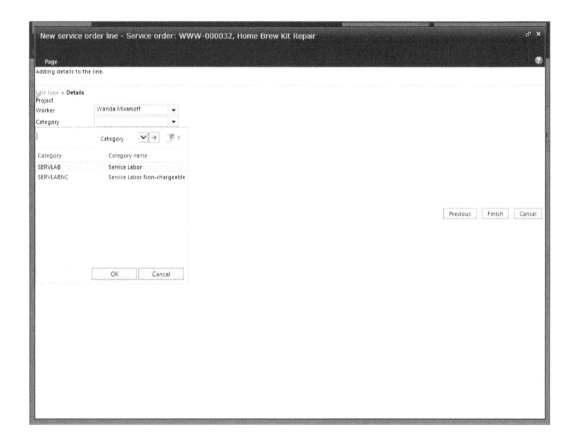

This will take you to the line detail entry form where you can select the same **Category** as you entered in the previous screen.

Posting Through The Service Management Portal

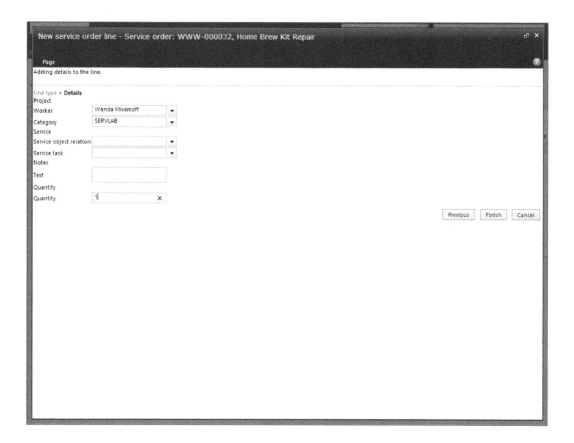

And then you can specify the **Quantity** that you want to post to the **Service Order**.

Posting Through The Service Management Portal

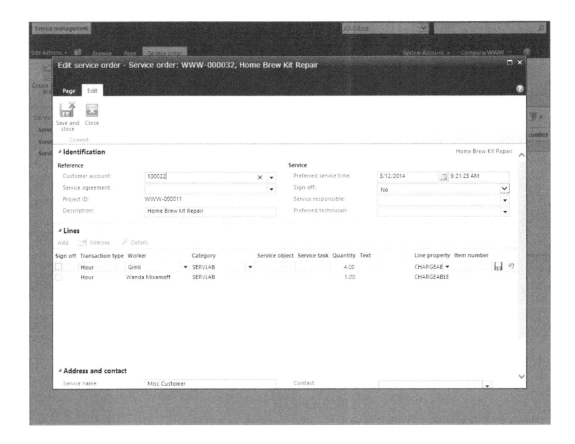

When you are done, all you need to do is click on the **Save and Close** button in the ribbon bar to save the new information.

Posting Material To Service Orders

You can also post material to the **Service Orders** in the same way that you posted time.

Posting Material To Service Orders

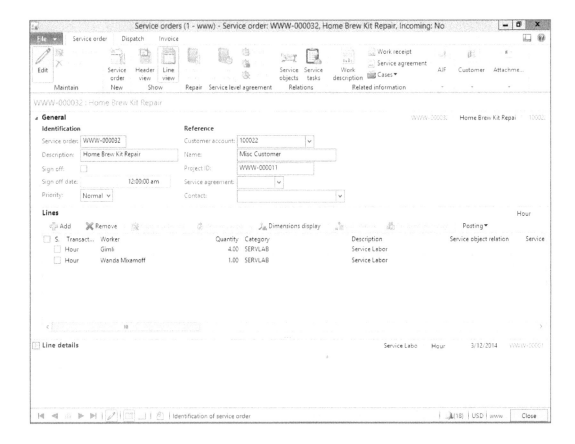

From within the **Lines** tab on the **Service order** click on the **Add** button in the tool bar to create a new service order line.

Posting Material To Service Orders

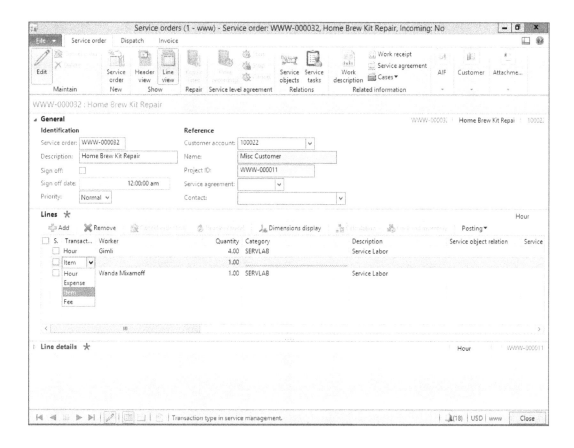

To post materials against the **Service Order** select **Item** from the **Transaction type** drop down.

Posting Material To Service Orders

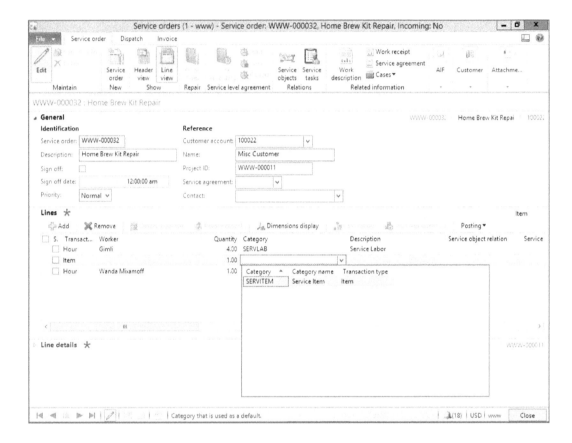

Enter in **Quantity** that you want to post and then select the **Category** that you want to use for this line item.

Posting Material To Service Orders

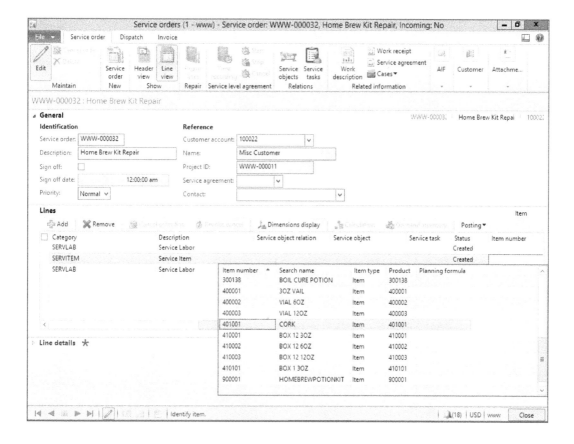

Then select the **Item Number** from the list box for the material that you want to issue to the **Service Order**.

Posting Material To Service Orders

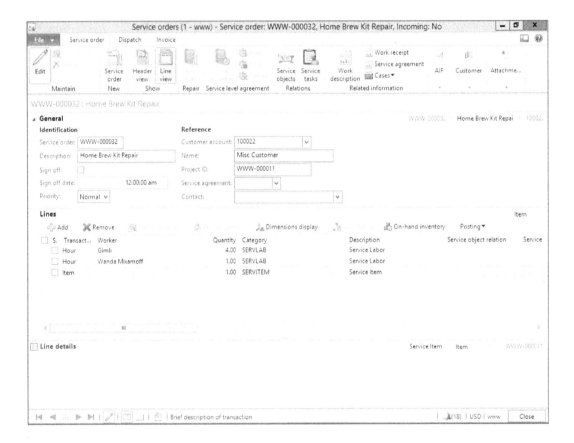

After you have done that, you can save the **Service Order** to update the record.

Signing Off and Posting Service Order Lines

Once you have entered time and materials against a **Service Order** you can approve the lines by signing off on them, and also post the lines to the project allowing them to be tracked and also invoiced.

Signing Off and Posting Service Order Lines

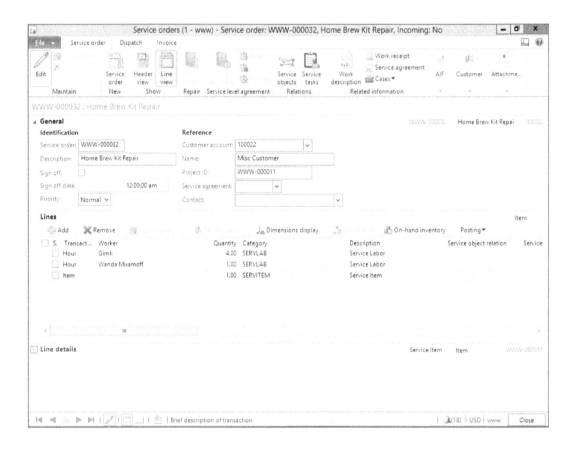

Select any of the lines that you want to approve for posting, and expand the **Line details** tab so that you can see the **General** subtab.

Signing Off and Posting Service Order Lines

If you want to approve just a single line, then you just have to check the **Sign off** check box against the line of the **Service Order**.

Signing Off and Posting Service Order Lines

Alternatively, if you want to approve all of the lines that were posted to the **Service Order** then you can check the **Signoff** box within the header, and it will sign off all the child lines.

Signing Off and Posting Service Order Lines

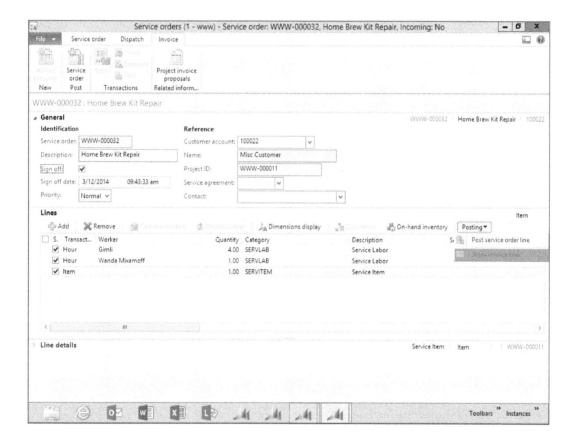

Once the line has been approved, you will be able to select the **Post service order line** option from the **Postings** drop down menu within the **Lines** group.

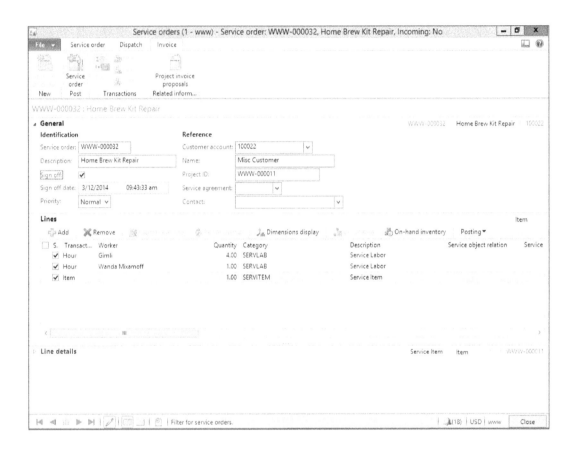

If you want to post all of the lines that you have signed off on through it may be easier to select the **Service Order** menu button within the **Post** group of the **Invoice** tab of the Service Order.

Signing Off and Posting Service Order Lines

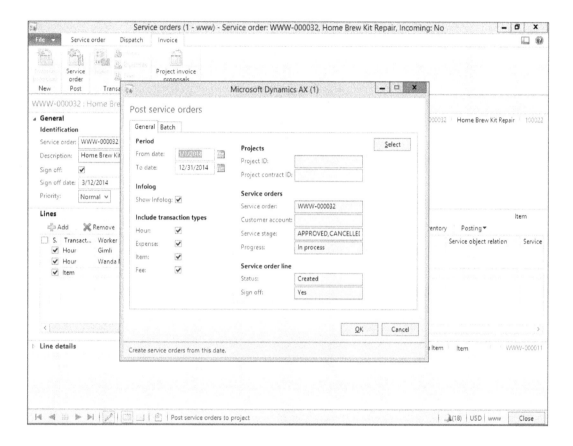

When the **Post service orders** dialog box is displayed, select a to and from date that you want to capture the time and materials from, and also check the transactions that you want to include in the postings.

When you are ready to post the lines, click on the **OK** button.

Signing Off and Posting Service Order Lines

If there are unposted transactions, then you will receive an Infolog that tells you that they have been posted to a journal.

Creating An Invoice Proposal From The Service Order

Once you have time and material posted against a **Service Order**, then you can start the billing process for the services by creating an **Invoice Proposal**. This will later be turned into a Receivables Invoice for the customer.

Creating An Invoice Proposal From The Service Order

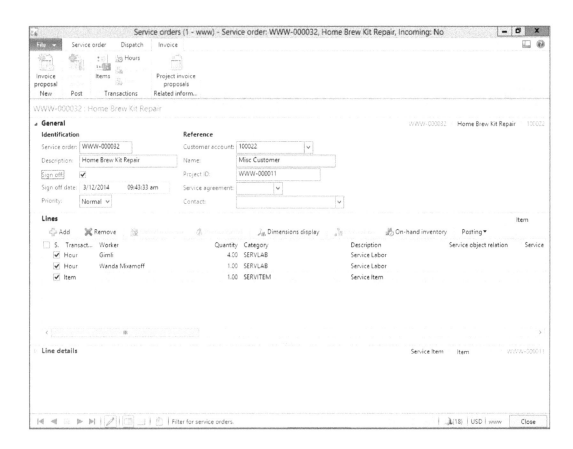

Open up the **Service Order** that you want to create the **Invoice Proposal** for and click on the **Invoice Proposal** button within the **New** group of the **Invoice** ribbon bar.

Creating An Invoice Proposal From The Service Order

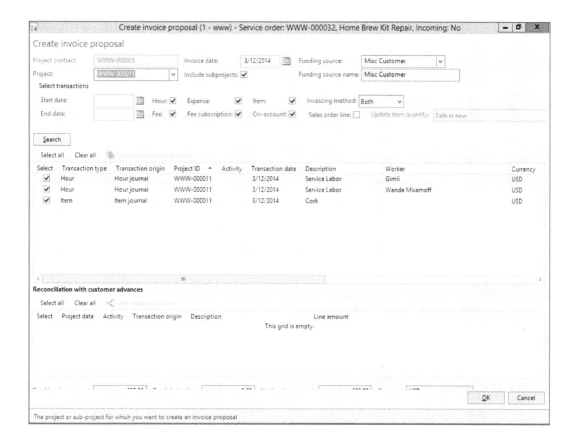

When the **Create Invoice Proposal** dialog box is displayed, you can select the signed-off lines that you want to create the **Invoice Proposal** for and then click the **OK** button.

Creating An Invoice Proposal From The Service Order

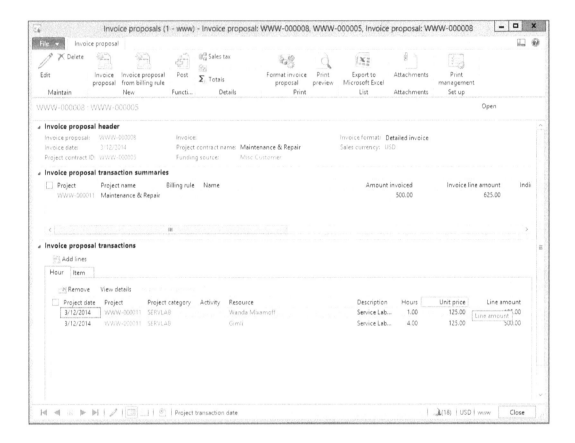

This will create an **Invoice Proposal** for you and open up the **Invoice Proposal** maintenance form.

Notice that the time and material have been split out into their own detail tabs. If you select the **Hours** tab then you will see all of the proposed time.

Creating An Invoice Proposal From The Service Order

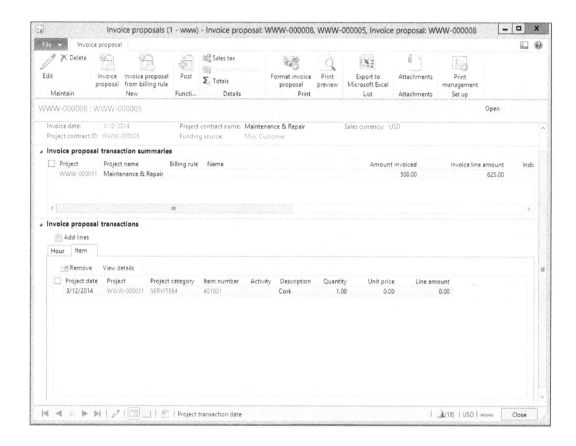

If you click on the **Items** tab, then you will see all of the proposed material lines.

Creating An Invoice Proposal From The Service Order

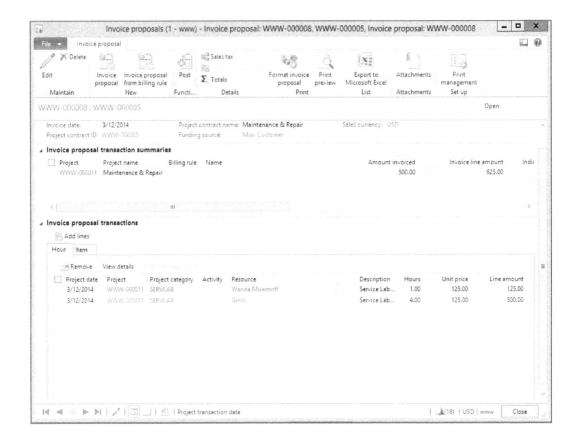

To convert the **Invoice Proposal** to a receivables invoice, just click on the **Post** menu button within the **Functions** group of the **Invoice Proposal** ribbon bar.

Creating An Invoice Proposal From The Service Order

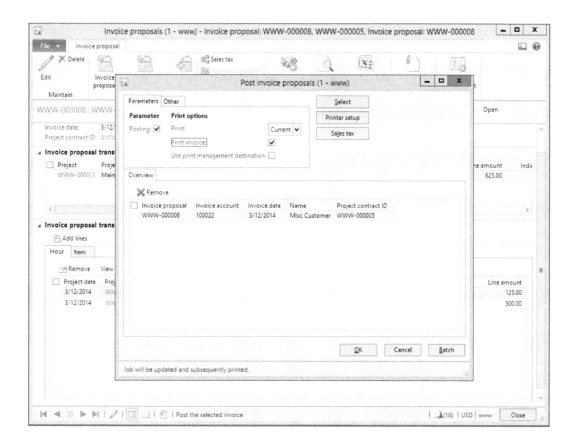

When the **Post Invoice Proposals** dialog box is displayed, just click on the **OK** button.

Creating An Invoice Proposal From The Service Order

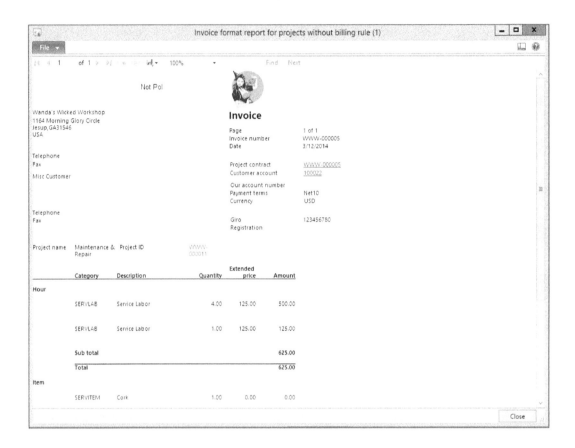

If you have the **Print Invoice** flag set, then it will also create the invoice for you and either print to the screen, or email it to the customer depending on your print management settings.

Creating Project Statements for Service Orders

As you start accruing time and expenses against your **Service Orders** you can take advantage of the **Project Statements** function within the **Projects** to track how much the agreement is costing, and if you are breaking even.

In this example we will show how you can run a **Project Statement** for a service agreement to analyze the profitability.

Creating Project Statements for Service Orders

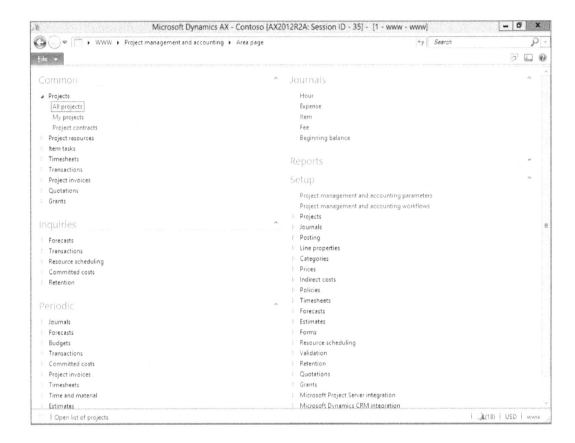

From the **Project management and accounting** area page, select the **All projects** menu item from within the **Projects** folder of the **Common** group.

Creating Project Statements for Service Orders

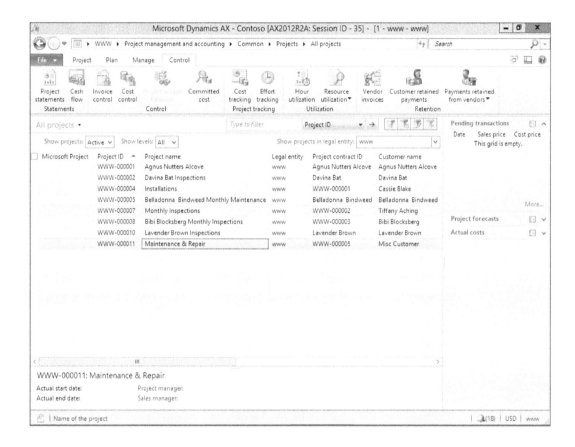

Click on the **Project Statements** button within the **Statements** group of the **Control** ribbon bar.

Creating Project Statements for Service Orders

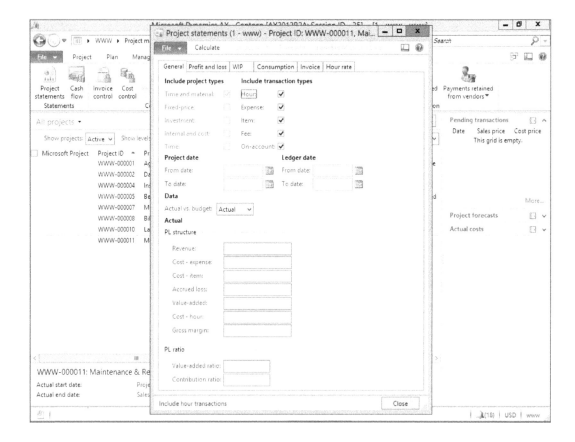

The first time that the **Project Statements** dialog box is displayed for a project, it will not show any information. To populate the statement, specify the from and to dates for the statement and then click on the **Calculate** option in the menu bar.

Creating Project Statements for Service Orders

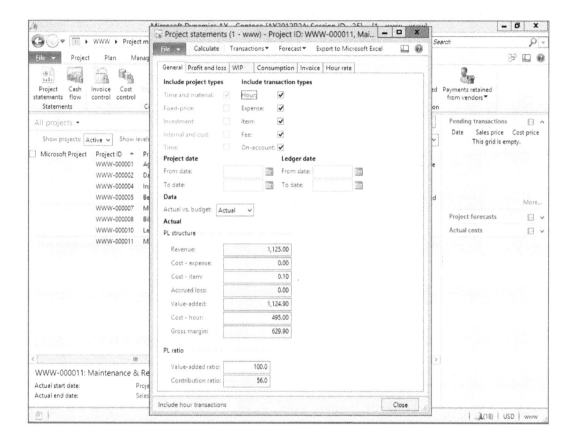

The system will now show you a break down on all of the costs and revenue for the project.

Creating Project Statements for Service Orders

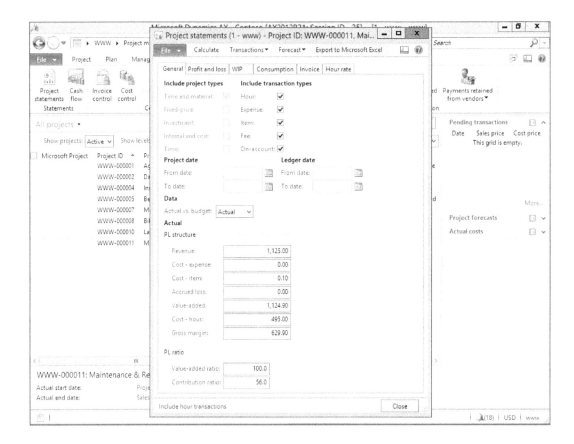

You can also create a pivot table view of this data within Excel by clicking on the **Export to Microsoft Excel** button in the menu bar.

Creating Project Statements for Service Orders

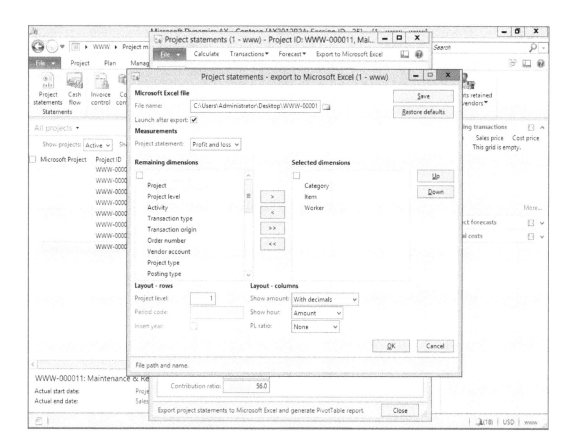

When the Export dialog box is displayed, specify a file location for the statement, select the dimensions that you want to export to Excel, and then click on the **OK** button.

Creating Project Statements for Service Orders

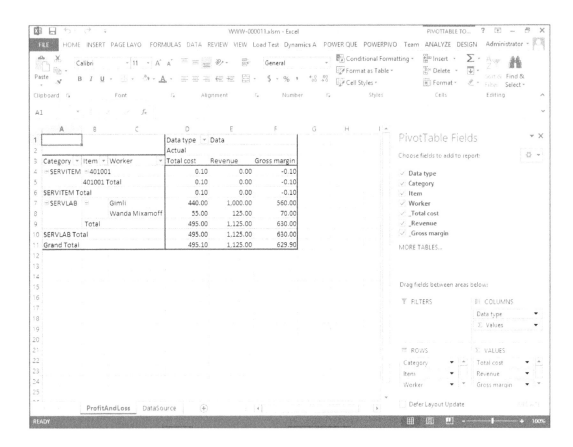

This will create a Statement for your project within Excel.

Very cool.

Viewing Posted Transactions Against Your Projects

Once your transactions have been posted, you can view them against the projects that are associated with the **Service Agreement**.

In this example we will show how you can view your **Service Order** transactions through **Projects**.

Viewing Posted Transactions Against Your Projects

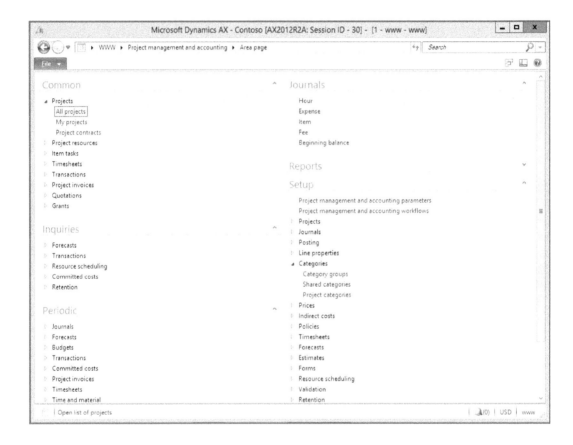

From the **Project management and accounting** area page, select the **All projects** menu item from within the **Projects** folder of the **Common** group.

Viewing Posted Transactions Against Your Projects

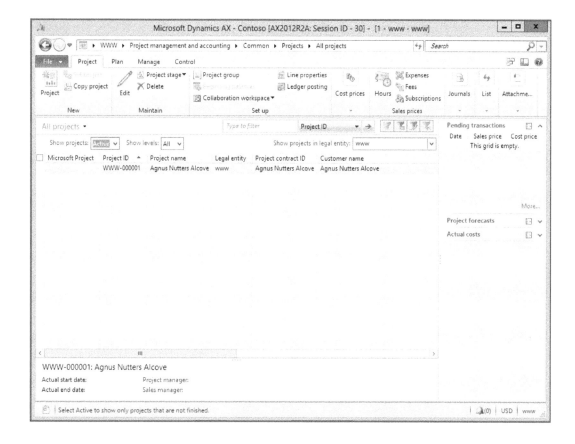

Select the project that is associated with your **Service Agreement**.

Viewing Posted Transactions Against Your Projects

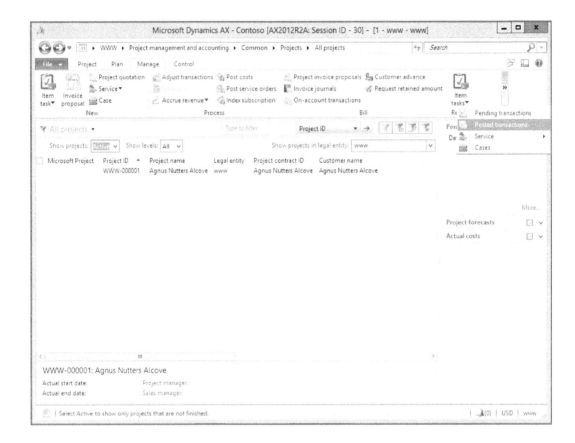

From the **Manage** ribbon bar, click on the **Posted transactions** menu item within the **Related information** group.

Viewing Posted Transactions Against Your Projects

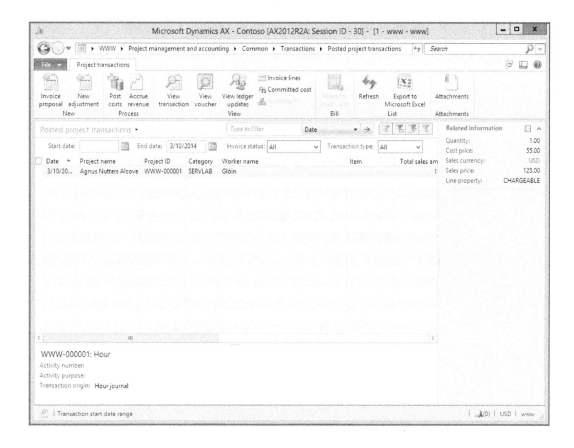

This will show you all of the transactions that have been transferred from the **Service Order** over to the **Project.**

Viewing Posted Transactions Against Your Projects

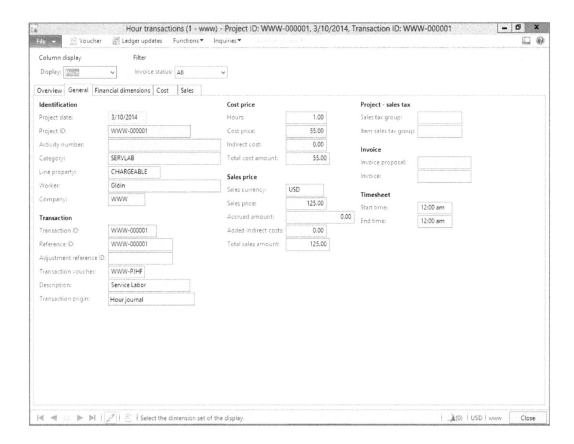

Drilling into the record will show you more information about the line item.

Invoicing Service Orders Time & Material Through Projects

Once you have posted the transactions to your **Service Order Project** you can use the **Invoice Proposal** function to automatically generate the invoice transactions for the customer so that they can be processed by the receivables department.

In this example we will show how you can generate and post an Invoice Proposal.

Invoicing Service Orders Time & Material Through Projects

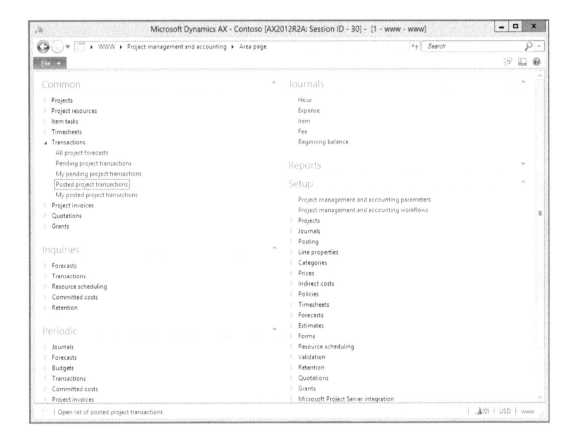

From the **Project management and accounting** area page, select the **Posted project transactions** menu item from within the **Transactions** folder of the **Common** group.

Invoicing Service Orders Time & Material Through Projects

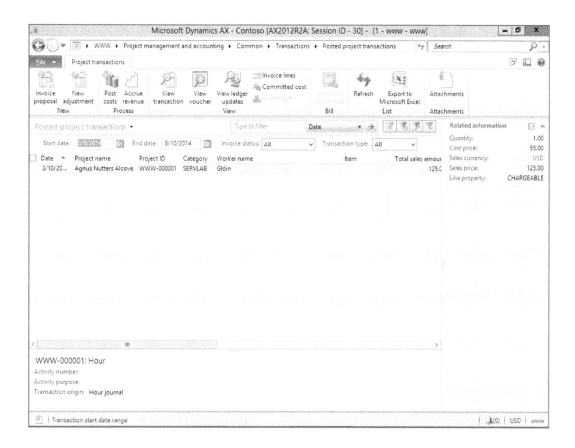

This will show you a list of all the transactions posted through the Projects.

From the **New** group of the **Project transactions** ribbon bar, click on the **Invoice proposal** button.

Invoicing Service Orders Time & Material Through Projects

When the **Create invoice proposal** dialog appears, it will show all of the uninvoiced transactions. To create the invoice proposals, just click on the **OK** button.

Invoicing Service Orders Time & Material Through Projects

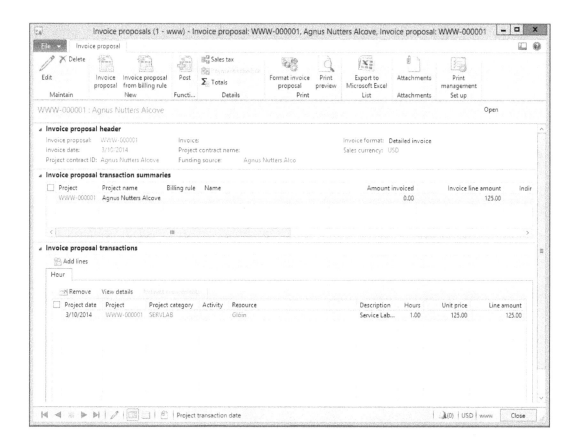

You will now be taken to the **Invoice proposal** that was created from the transactions. To convert the **Invoice proposal** into an **AR Invoice** click on the **Post** button within the **Functions** group of the **Invoice proposal** ribbon bar.

Invoicing Service Orders Time & Material Through Projects

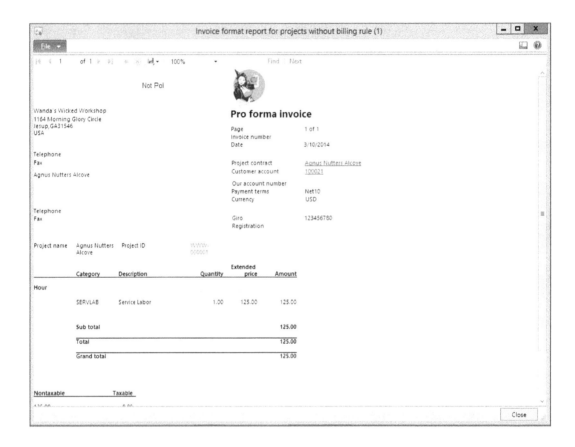

Print Preview

Invoicing Service Orders Time & Material Through Projects

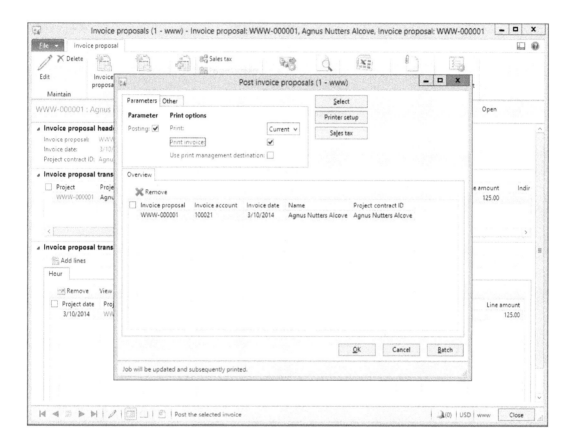

If you want to Print the Invoice, then you can check the option on the Posting dialog box. When you are ready to post, click the **OK** button.

Invoicing Service Orders Time & Material Through Projects

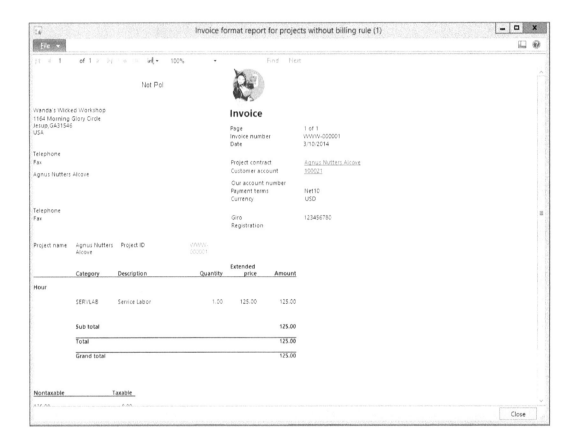

The Invoice Posting process will show you the invoice that is generated. You can automatically email this to your customer as well through the print management function.

Invoicing Service Orders Time & Material Through Projects

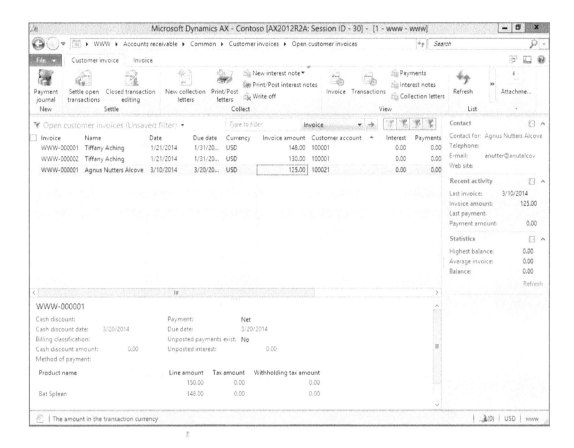

If you look within the Receivables area, you will also see the invoice transaction has now been added to the customer account.

Invoicing Service Orders Time & Material Through Projects

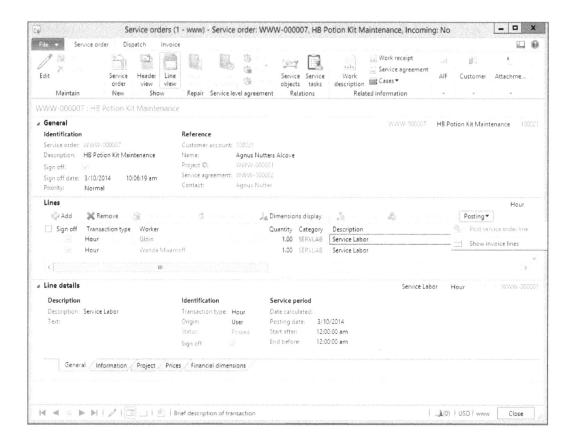

Also, if you are on the **Service Order** then you can see the invoices that are associated with the lines by clicking on the **Postings** menu item within the **Lines** tab, and selecting the **Show Invoice Lines** submenu.

Invoicing Service Orders Time & Material Through Projects

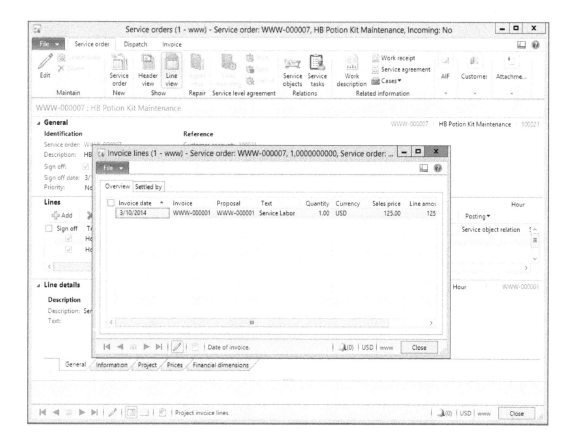

This will open up a dialog box that shows you all of the Invoice lines that are associated with the service order lines.

SERVICE
AGREEMENTS

You can streamline the **Service Order** creation process within **Service Management** by creating **Service Agreements**. These are templates that are associated with customers that also allow you to automatically create **Service Orders** based on the agreement that you have with the customer.

Creating a Service Agreement

Service Agreements are the basis for all of your service order creation. They allow you to define the default structures of your **Service Orders** and also link back to the project management area so that you are able to bill for any activity that has been performed against the service orders. As a result, the first step in the process of configuring **Service Management** is to create a **Service Agreement.**

Creating a Service Agreement

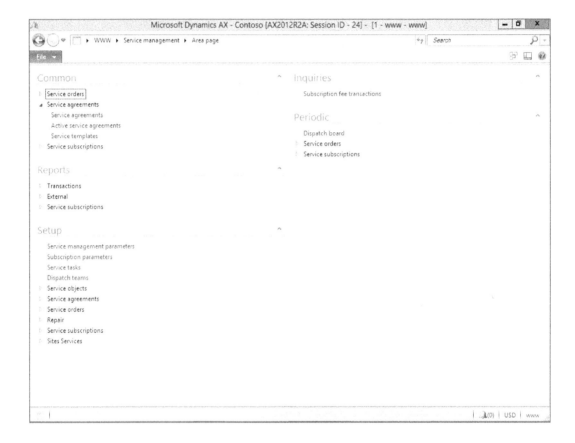

From the **Service Management** area page, select the **Service agreements** menu item from within the **Service agreements** folder of the **Common** group.

Creating a Service Agreement

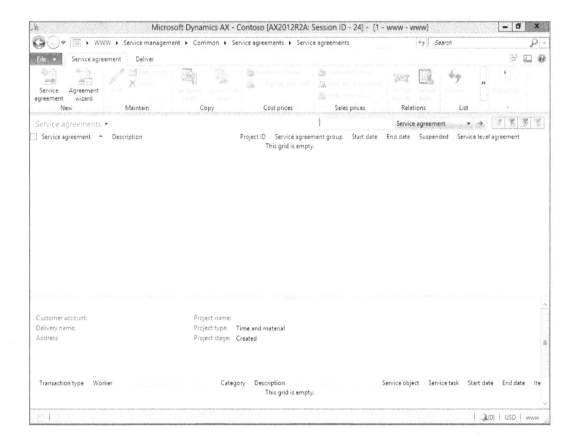

When the **Service Agreements** list page opens up, click on the **Agreement wizard** button within the **New** group of the **Service agreement** ribbon bar.

Creating a Service Agreement

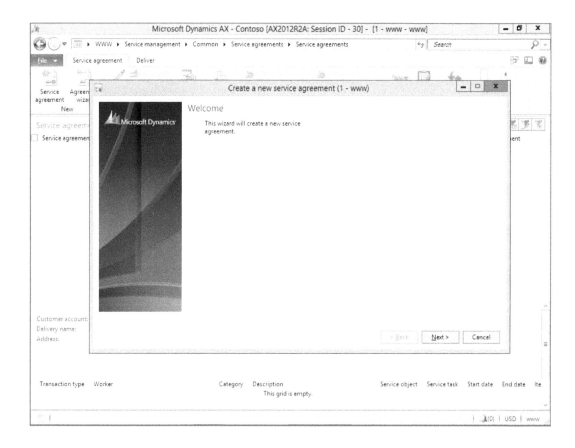

When the **Service Agreement** wizard is displayed, click then **Next** button to start the process.

Creating a Service Agreement

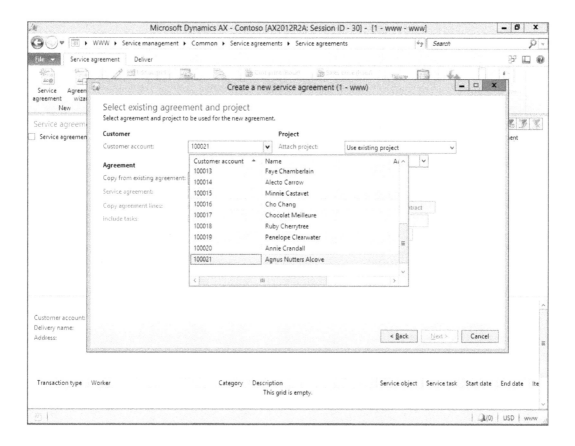

Select the **Customer account** that you would like the service agreement to be associated with.

Creating a Service Agreement

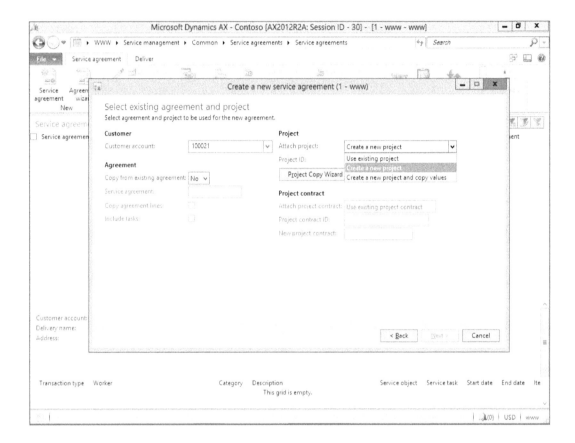

Then select the *Create a new project* option from the **Attach project** drop down to tell the system that we want to create an entirely new project to track this information.

Note: If you have already created a project for the customer, and would like to mingle the Service Agreements, then you can select the *Use existing project* option.

Creating a Service Agreement

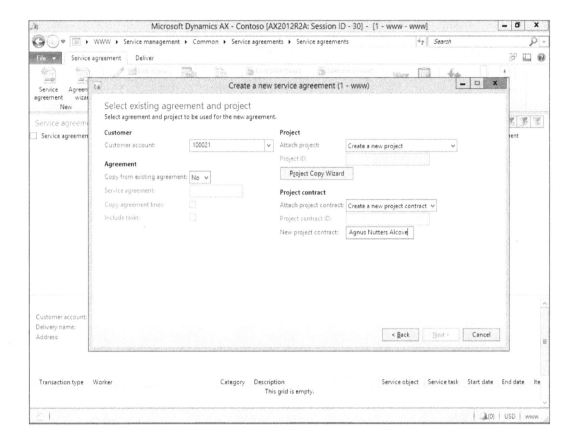

Within the **Project contract** group, enter a description of the Service Agreement into the **New project contract** field.

When you have done this, click on the **Next** button to move to the next step in the wizard.

Creating a Service Agreement

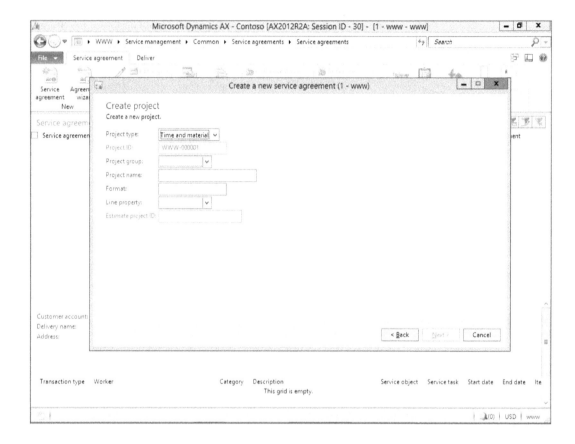

Creating a Service Agreement

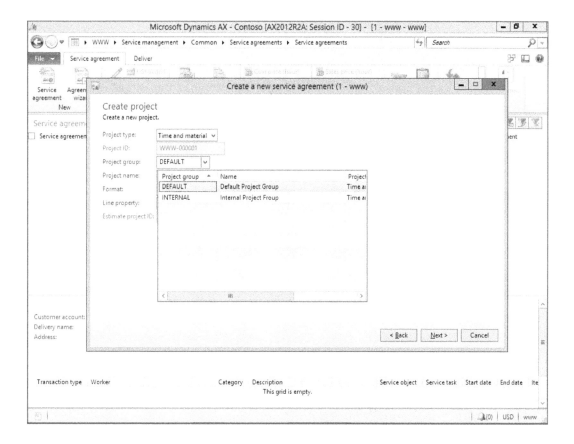

Creating a Service Agreement

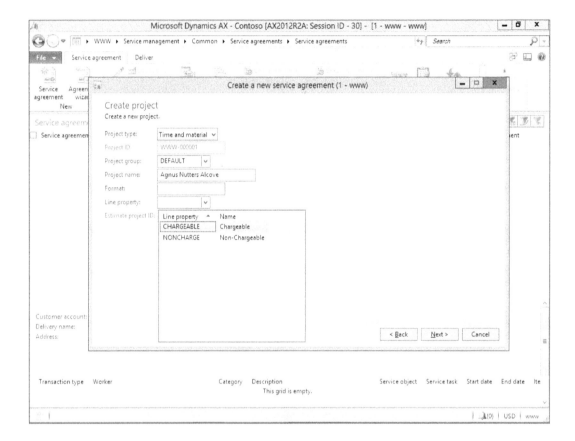

For the new project creation defaults, select *Time and material* for the **Project Type**.

Select a **Project group**.

Enter the name of the Service Agreement into the **Project name** field so that we can easily trace the project back to the agreement.

Finally set the default **Line property**. In this case we want all lines to be chargeable unless we override the value.

Creating a Service Agreement

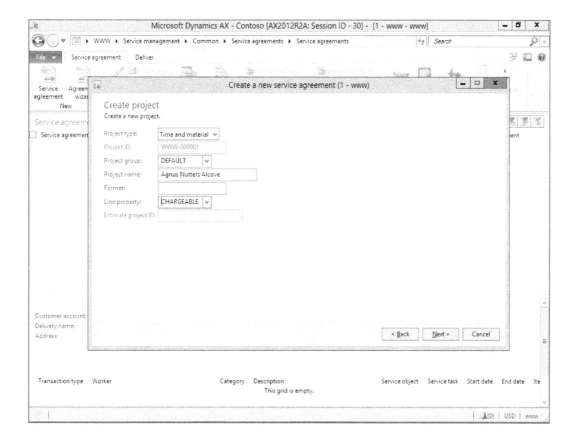

When the project defaults have been defined click on the **Next** button to continue to the next step.

Creating a Service Agreement

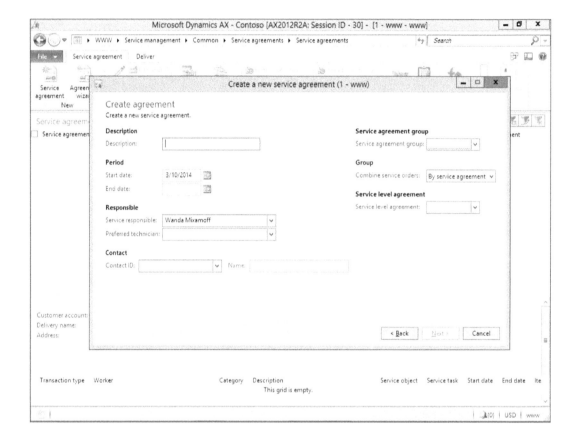

The next step is to define the **Service Agreement**.

Enter a **Description** for the Service Agreement.

Creating a Service Agreement

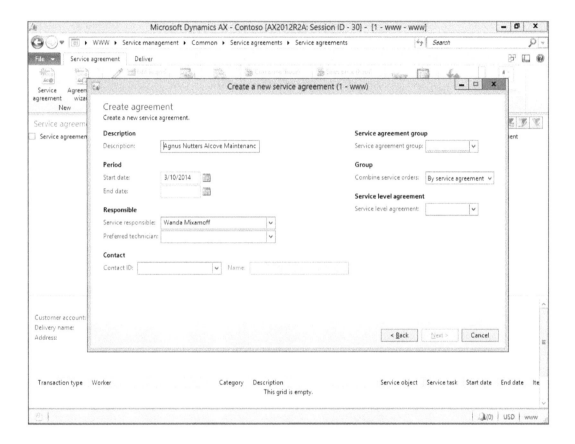

Enter a date into the **Start date** field to specify when you want the agreement to be effective.

Creating a Service Agreement

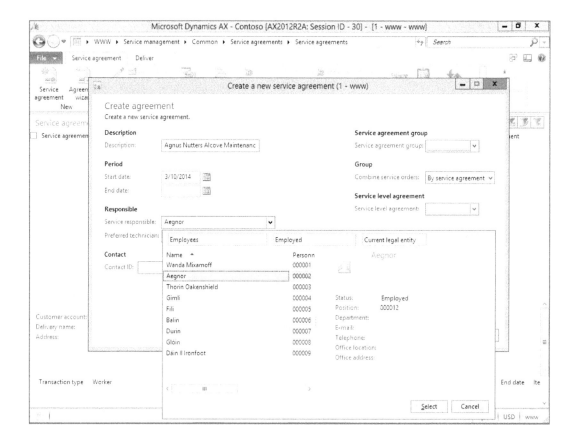

If you want to have default service technicians to be associated with this **Service Agreement** then you can also specify those here as well.

Creating a Service Agreement

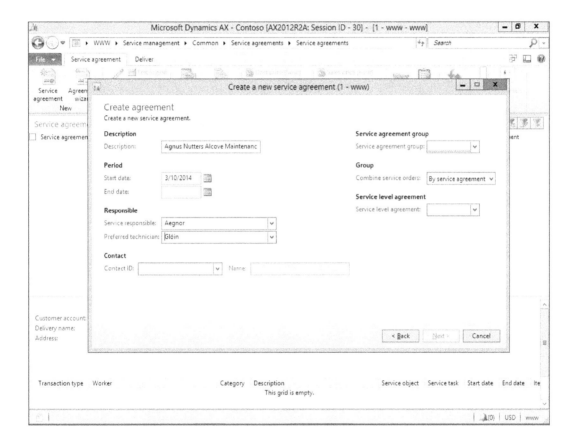

Creating a Service Agreement

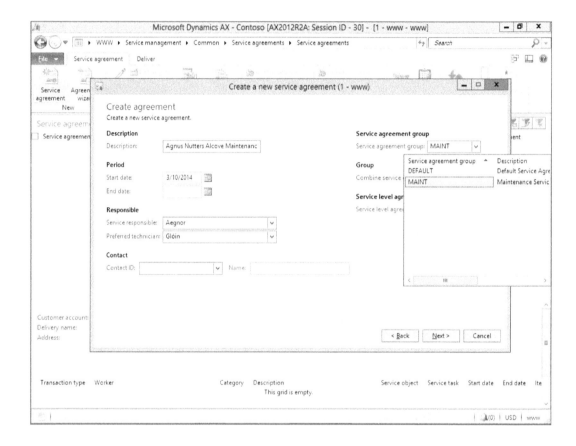

And then select the default **Service Agreement Group** that you want to use to classify your Service Agreement and Orders.

Creating a Service Agreement

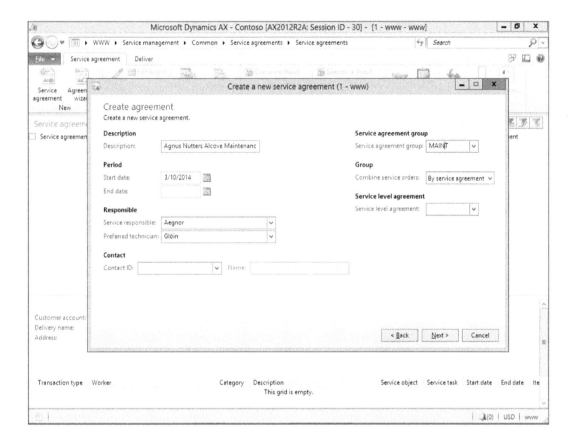

When you have configures the defaults for the **Service Agreement** click the **Next** button to continue on.

Creating a Service Agreement

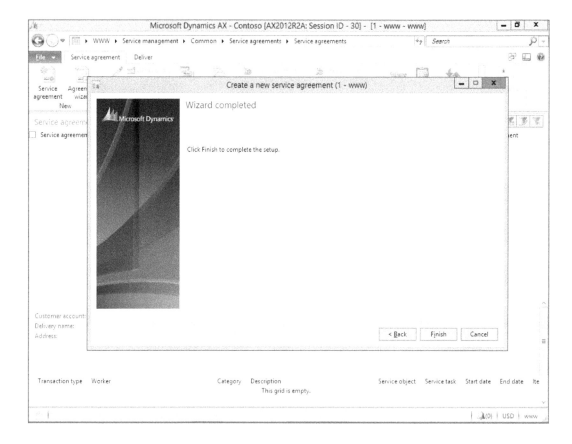

When you reach the confirmation page, click the **Finish** button to have the system create your **Service Agreement**.

Creating a Service Agreement

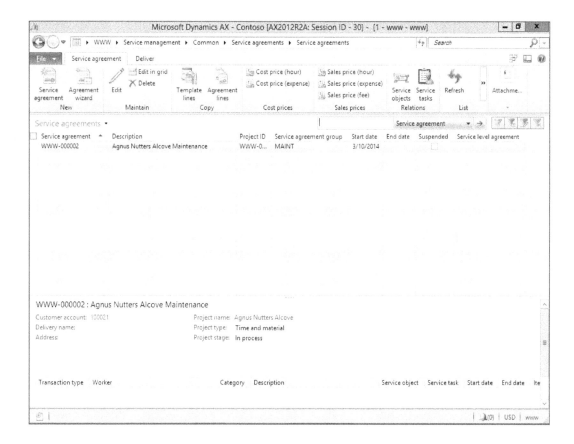

Now you will have a **Service Agreement** that you can start using.

Assigning Valid Service Tasks to Agreements

Once you have defined your **Service Tasks** you can start assigning them to your **Service Agreement** and **Service Order** lines.

In this example we will show how to associate a **Service Task** to a **Service Agreement** line.

Assigning Valid Service Tasks to Agreements

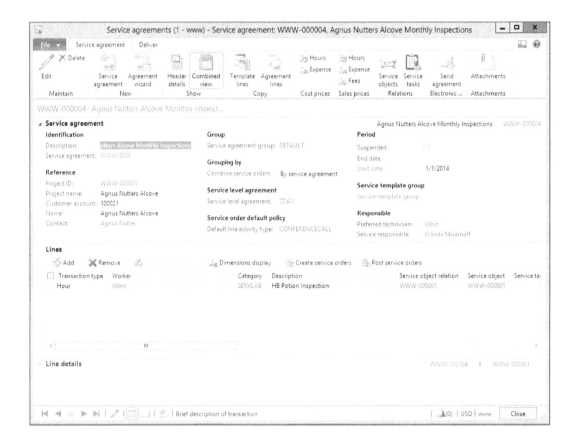

The first step is to associate a **Service Task** with your **Service Agreement**. To do this, open up your **Service Agreement** and then click on the **Service tasks** button within the **Relations** group of the **Service Agreement** ribbon bar.

Assigning Valid Service Tasks to Agreements

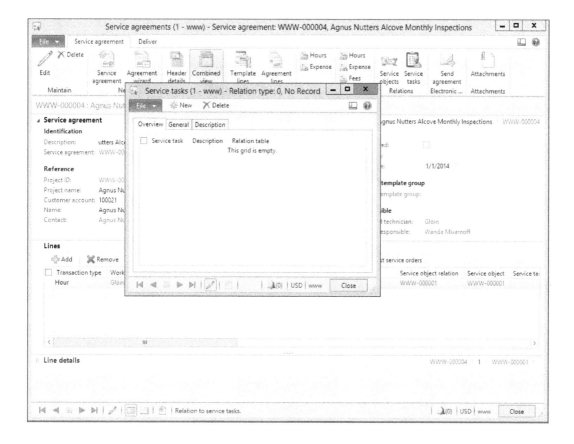

When the **Service Tasks** maintenance form is displayed, click on the **New** button in the menu bar to create a new record.

Assigning Valid Service Tasks to Agreements

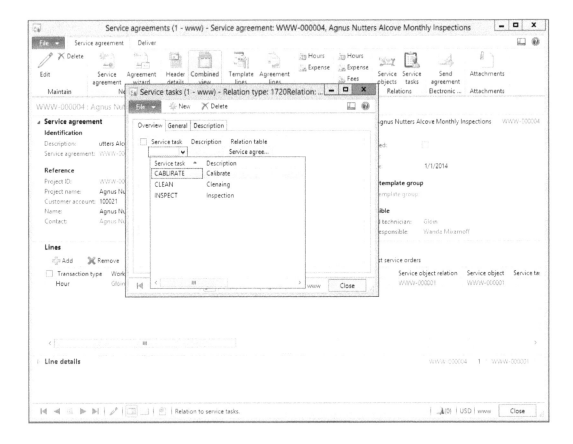

From the **Service task** dropdown box, select the **Service tasks** that you configured in the previous step.

Assigning Valid Service Tasks to Agreements

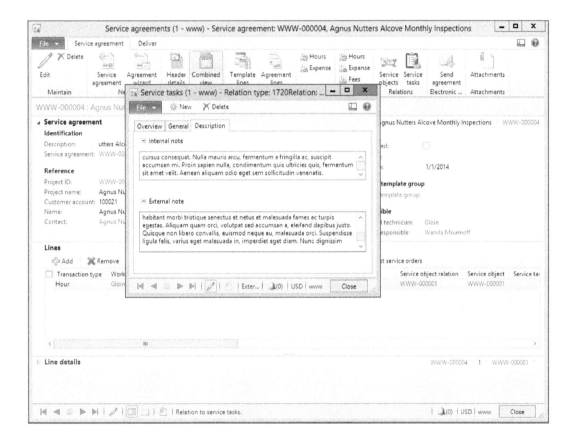

If you switch to the **Description** tab, you can also include internal and external comments and notes for the tasks.

Assigning Valid Service Tasks to Agreements

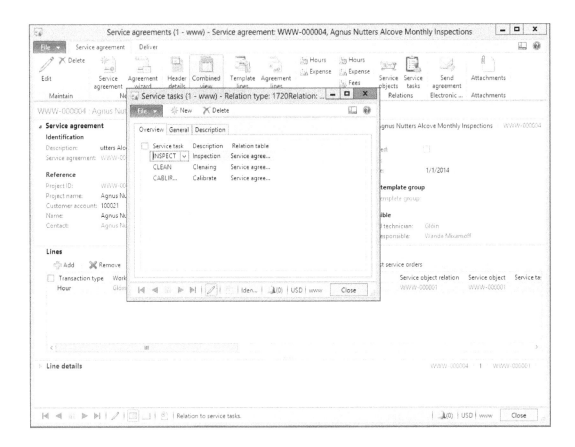

You can continue adding **Service tasks** to the **Service Agreement**.

When you are done, click on the **Close** button to exit the form.

Assigning Valid Service Tasks to Agreements

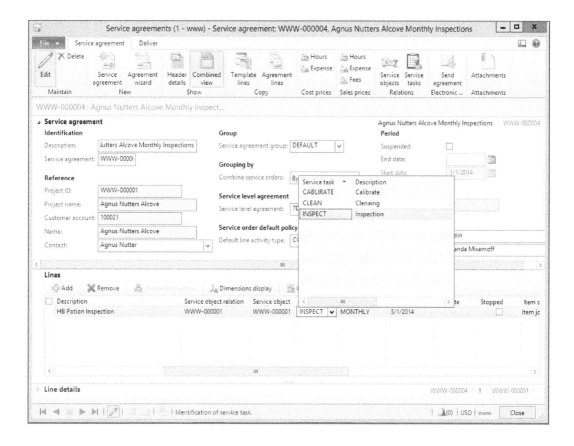

Now you will be able to associate the **Service task** with any of the lines on your **Service Agreement** and get better reporting.

Assigning Valid Service Tasks to Agreements

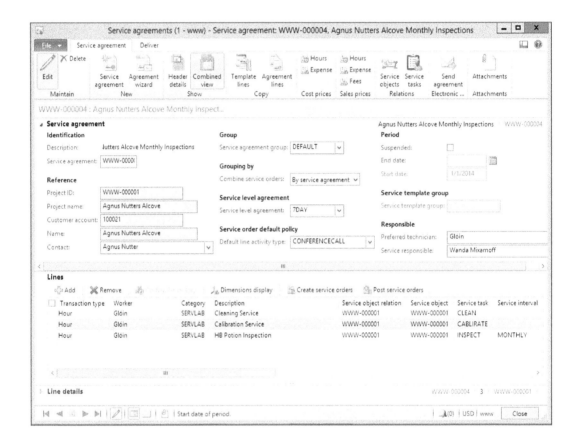

Note: If you add multiple lines to your **Service Agreement** then you can start differentiating the tasks that are being performed.

Creating a Service Order From A Service Agreement

Once you have a **Service Agreement** you can start creating **Service Orders** and posting time and material against them.

In this example we will show how you can create a **Service Order**.

Creating a Service Order From A Service Agreement

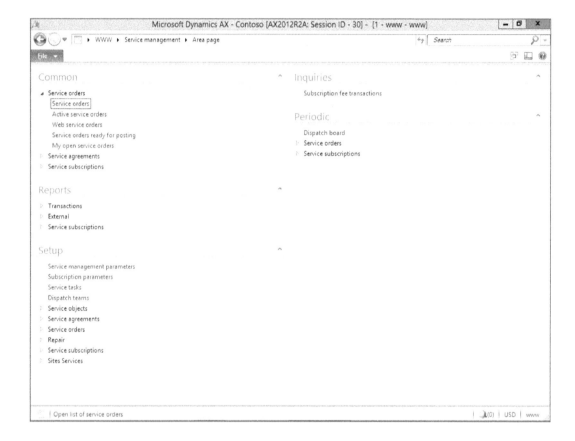

From the **Service Management** area page, select the **Service orders** menu item from within the **Service orders** folder of the **Common** group.

Creating a Service Order From A Service Agreement

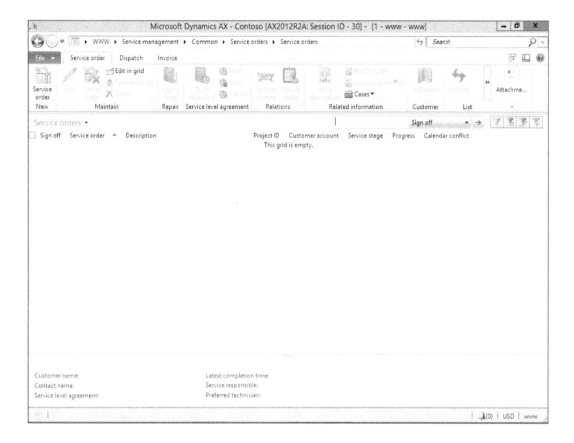

When the **Service Orders** list page opens up, click on the **Service order** button within the **New** group of the **Service order** ribbon bar.

Creating a Service Order From A Service Agreement

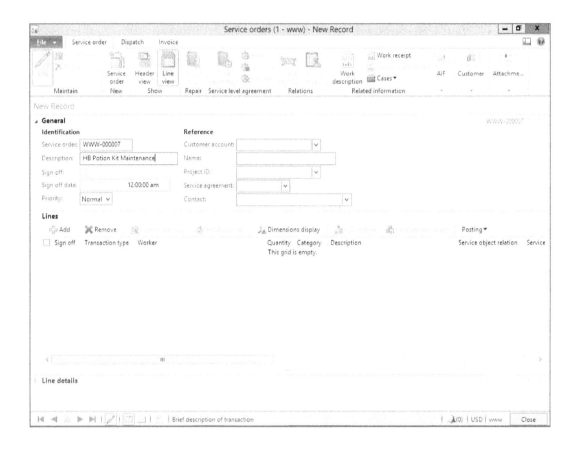

When the **Service** Orders maintenance form is displayed, enter a **Description**.

Creating a Service Order From A Service Agreement

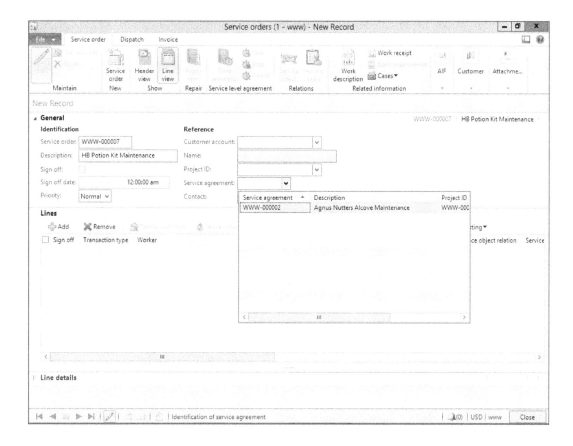

Within the **Reference** group select your **Service Agreement** that you set up in the previous step.

Creating a Service Order From A Service Agreement

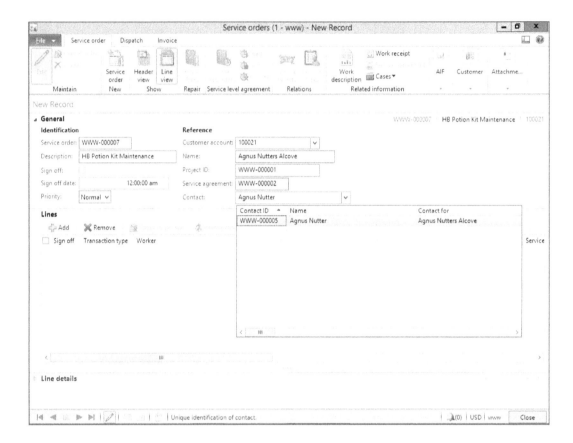

This will automatically default in the **Project** ID and the **Customer Account.**

If you want to specify a **Contact** for the Service order then you can select that from the dropdown.

Creating a Service Order From A Service Agreement

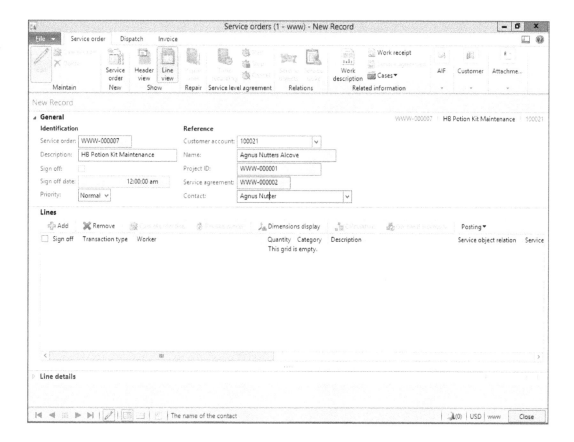

This will default in the **Customer account**, and the **Project ID** for you.

Alternatively, you can select the **Customer account** from the dropdown, and then select the **Service agreement** from the filtered list.

Creating Periodic Service Intervals

If you have service orders that repeat on a regular basis, then you can configure **Service Intervals** and then assign them to lines on your **Service Agreements** and then have the **Service Management** area automatically generate the Service Order jobs for you.

In this example we will show how you can define **Service Intervals** and adding them to **Service Agreement** lines.

Creating Periodic Service Intervals

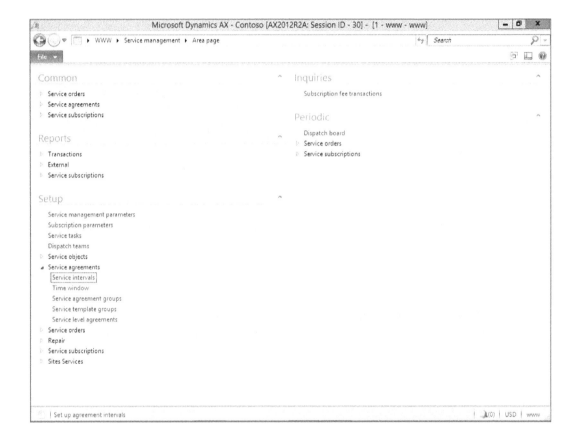

From the **Service management** area page, select the **Service intervals** menu item from within the **Service agreements** folder of the **Setup** group.

Creating Periodic Service Intervals

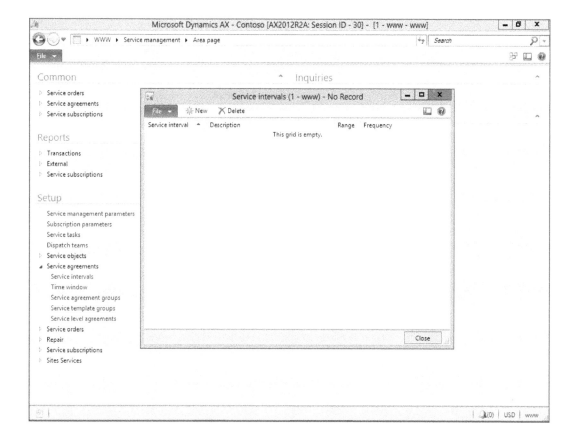

When the **Service Intervals** maintenance form is displayed, click on the **New** button in the menu bar to create a new record.

Creating Periodic Service Intervals

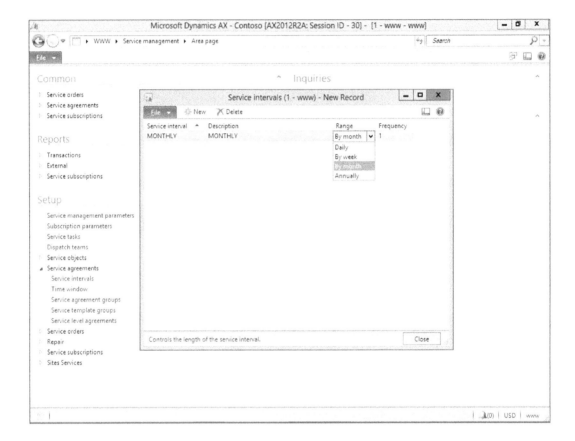

Assign a **Service Interval** code, and a **Description** and then from the **Range** dropdown, select the period type that you want to use for the **Frequency**.

Creating Periodic Service Intervals

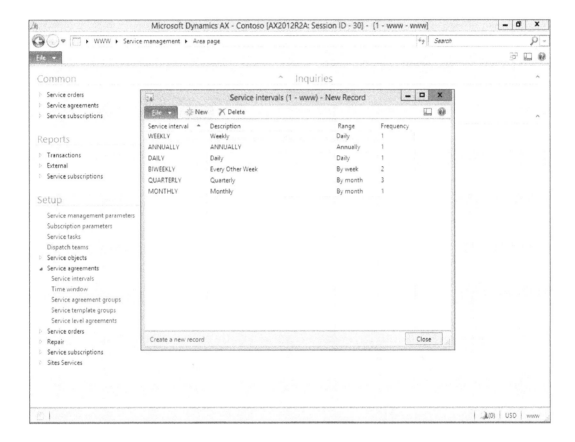

Repeat the steps for all of the different intervals that you would like to use, and when you are done, click the **Close** button to exit from the form.

Configuring Periodic Service Agreement Lines

You can use **Service Intervals** on **Service Agreement** lines to specify an how often you would like to have the system automatically create **Service Orders**. All you have to do is assign them to the lines.

Configuring Periodic Service Agreement Lines

To use the **Service Interval** open up your **Service Agreement** and add a new line. Within the **Service Interval** field, select the frequency that you want to perform the service order task.

Configuring Periodic Service Agreement Lines

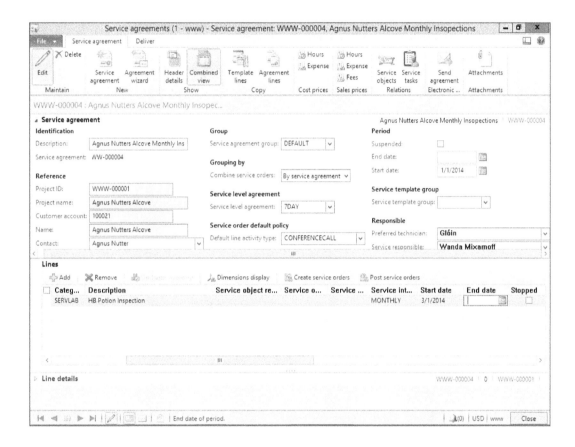

And then specify the start date for the task so that the frequency has a beginning.

Creating Periodic Service Orders

Once a **Service Agreement** tasks have been configured with a frequency, you can have the system automatically create the **Service Orders** for you through the periodic processing option.

In this example we will show how to get the system to create your scheduled **Service Orders** automatically.

Creating Periodic Service Orders

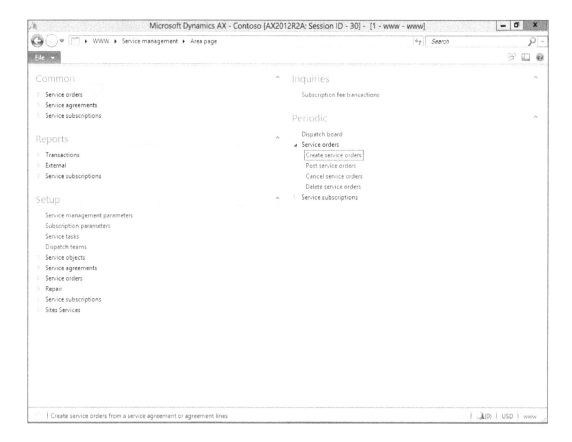

From the **Service management** area page, select the **Create service orders** menu item from within the **Service orders** folder of the **Periodic** group.

Creating Periodic Service Orders

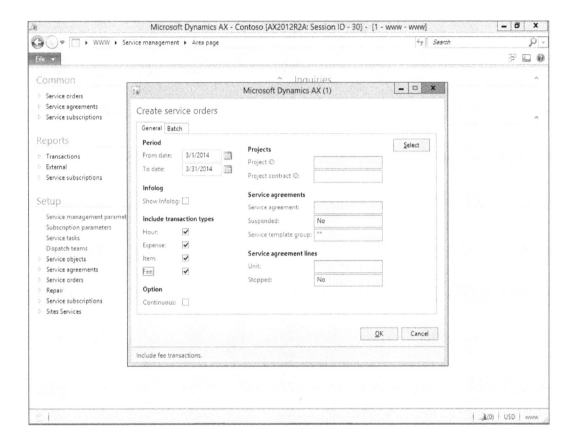

When the service order creation dialog box appears, select a to and from date that you want to search for recurring service order tasks, and also select the transaction types that you want to include. Then click the **OK** button.

Creating Periodic Service Orders

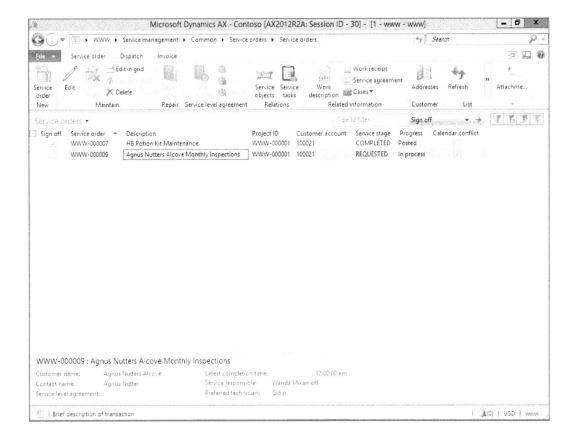

You will see the new **Service Orders** automatically show up.

Creating Periodic Service Orders

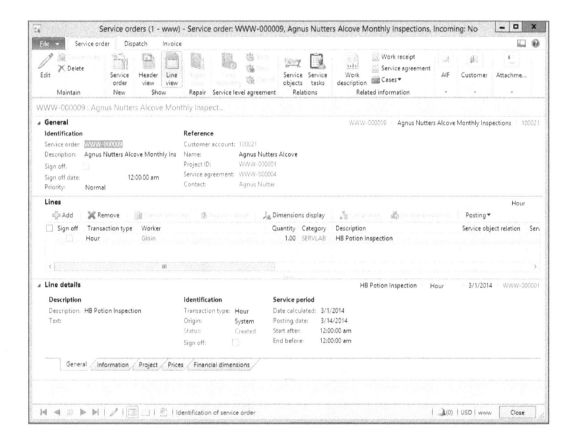

Drilling into the detail you will be able to see the task that was assigned to the work order.

SERVICE OBJECTS

If you want to track the products that you are performing **Service Orders** upon, then you will want to define **Service Objects** within the **Service Management** module. You will then be able to associate them with **Service Orders** and **Agreements**.

Creating Service Object Groups

In order to track all of your **Service Objects** you need to first create a **Service Order Group**. This will be used to group all of the common **Service Objects** together for management and reporting.

Creating Service Object Groups

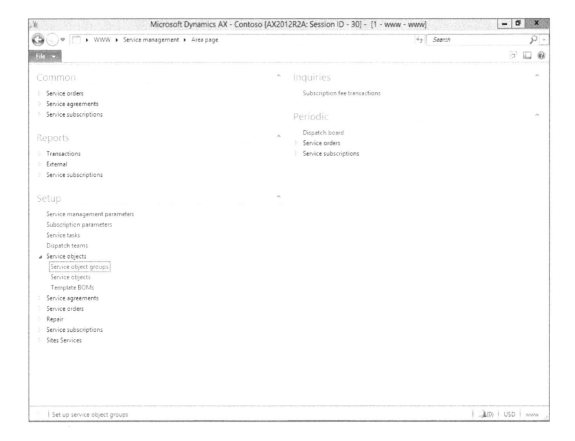

From the **Service management** area page, select the **Service object groups** menu item from within the **Service objects** folder of the **Setup** group.

Creating Service Object Groups

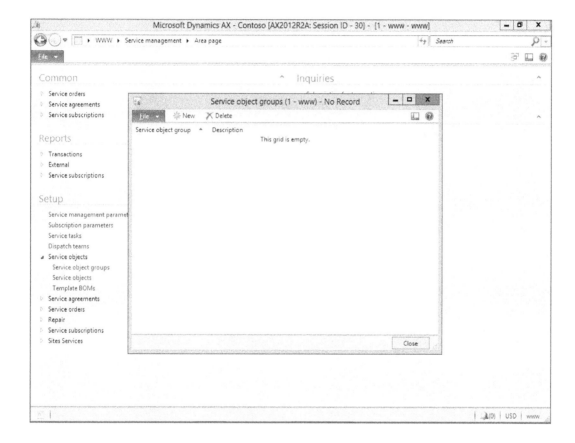

When the **Service Object Groups** maintenance form is displayed, click on the **New** button within the menu bar to create a new record.

Creating Service Object Groups

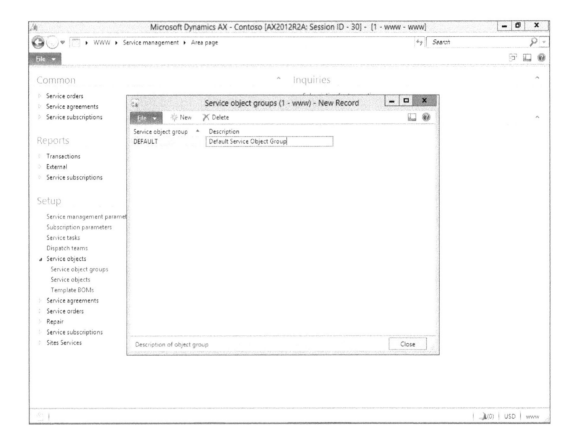

Then assign a code in the **Service Object Group** field, and a **Description.**

Creating Service Object Groups

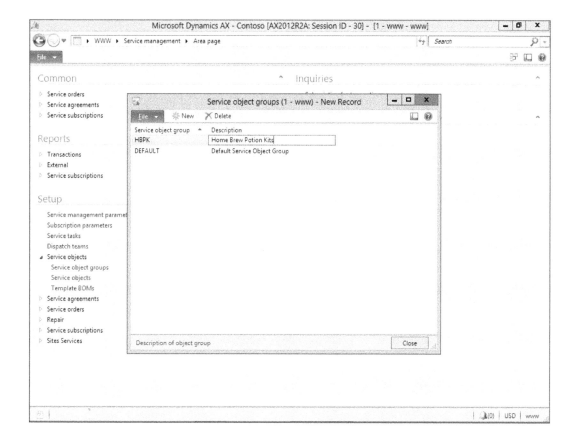

Repeat the steps for all of the different types of **Service Object Groups** that you want to track in the system.

Creating Service Objects

The **Service Management** area allows you to track what the **Service Orders** and **Service Agreements** are related to through what a called **Service Objects**. A Service Object could be something that is tracked as in inventoried item, or it could just be a reference to something that is being serviced.

Creating Service Objects

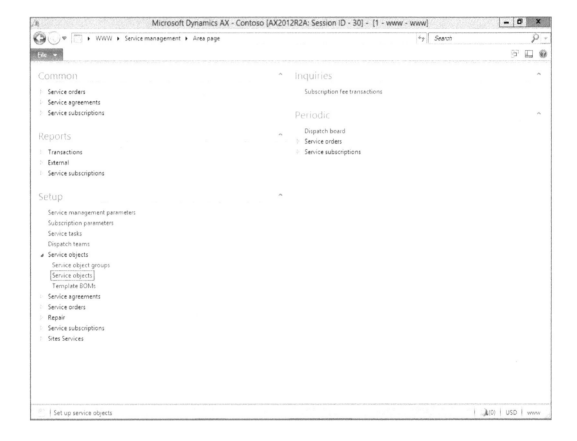

From the **Service management** area page, select the **Service objects** menu item from within the **Service objects** folder of the **Setup** group.

Creating Service Objects

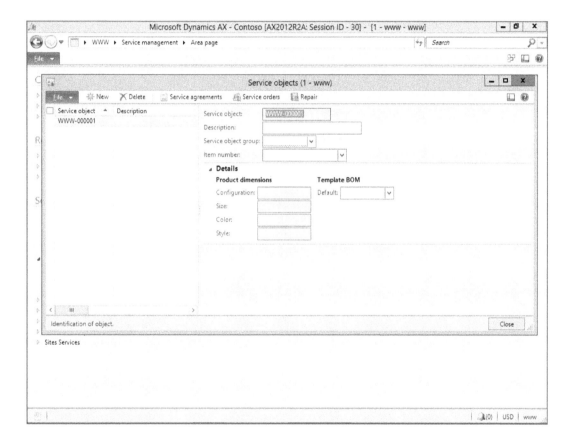

When the **Service objects** maintenance form is displayed, click on the **New** button in the menu bar to create a new record.

Creating Service Objects

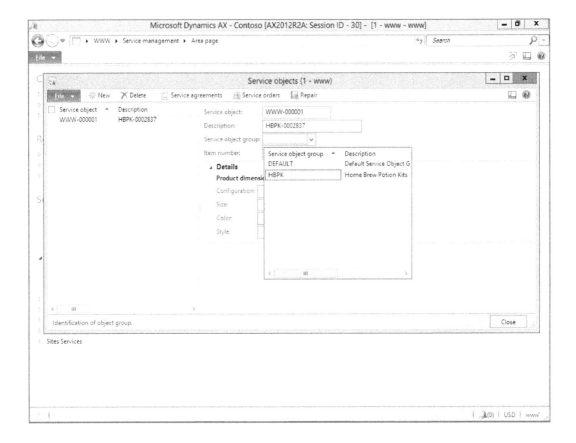

All you need to specify for the **Service Object** is the **Description** and the **Service object group**.

When you have defined all of your **Service Objects** click on the **Close** button to exit the form.

Creating Service Objects

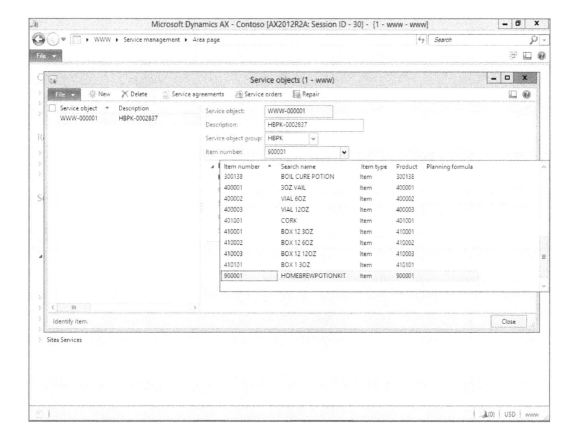

If you want to specify a tangible item with the **Service Object**, then select the **Item Number** from the dropdown list.

Creating Service Objects

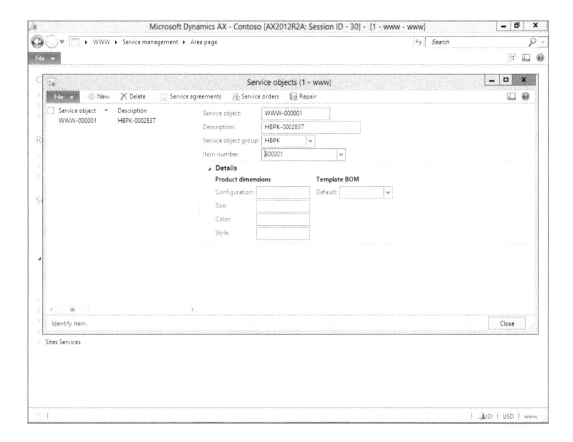

When you are done, just click on the **Close** button to exit from the form.

Assigning Service Objects to Service Agreements

Once you have defined your **Service Objects** you can start assigning them to your **Service Agreements** and **Service Orders**.

In this example we will show how to associate a **Service Object** to a **Service Agreement.**

Assigning Service Objects to Service Agreements

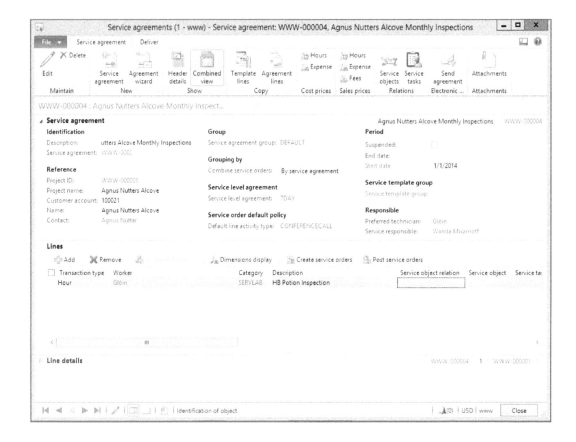

The first step is to associate a **Service Object** with your **Service Agreement**. To do this, open up your **Service Agreement** and then click on the **Service object** button within the **Relations** group of the **Service Agreement** ribbon bar.

Assigning Service Objects to Service Agreements

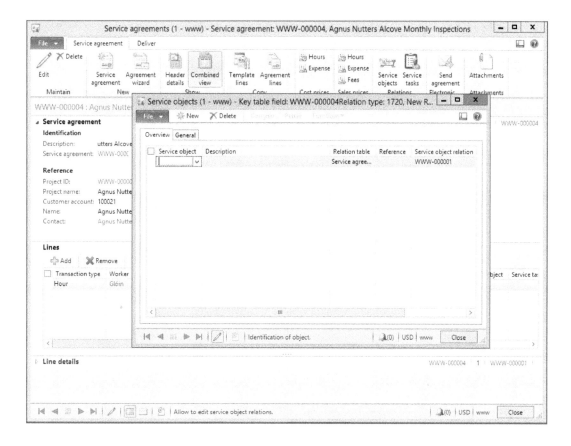

Then the **Service objects** maintenance form is displayed, click on the **New** button in the menu bar.

Assigning Service Objects to Service Agreements

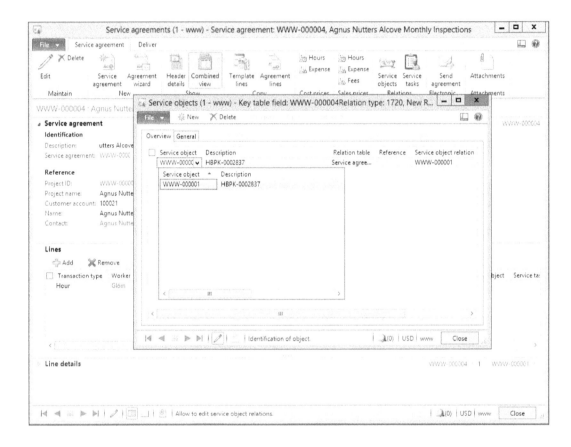

From the **Service Object** dropdown box, select the **Service Object** that you configured in the previous step.

Assigning Service Objects to Service Agreements

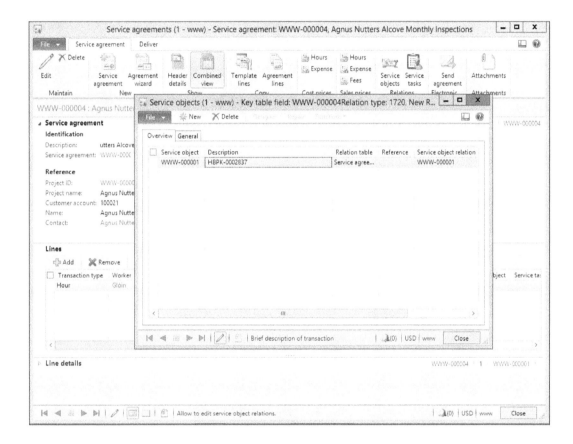

You can continue adding **Service Objects** to the **Service Agreement**.

When you are done, click on the **Close** button to exit the form.

Assigning Service Objects to Service Agreements

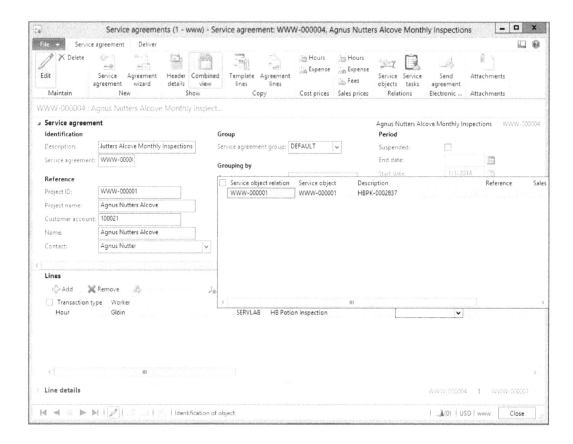

Now you will be able to associate the **Service Object** with any of the lines on your **Service Agreement** and get better reporting.

Assigning Service Objects to Service Agreements

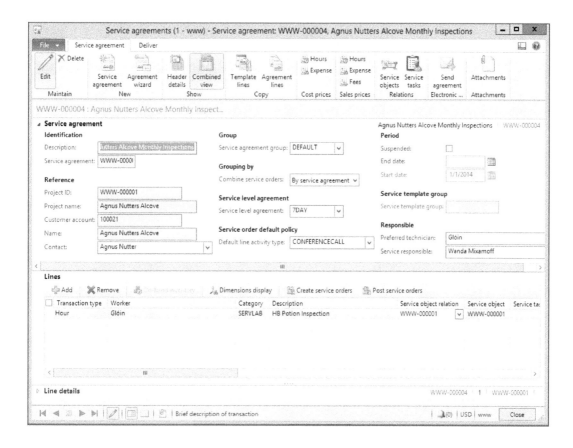

Now you have a **Service Object** associated with your **Service Agreement**.

REPAIR MANAGEMENT

The **Service Management** area also allows you to track repairs that have been performed as part of the **Service Order** process. Through this feature, you can track all of the symptoms reported by the customer, the diagnostics performed by the technician, and also the repair operations that are performed in order to fix the problems.

Defining Repair Conditions

The first part of this process allows you to define a set of **Repair Conditions** which are general repair categories.

Defining Repair Conditions

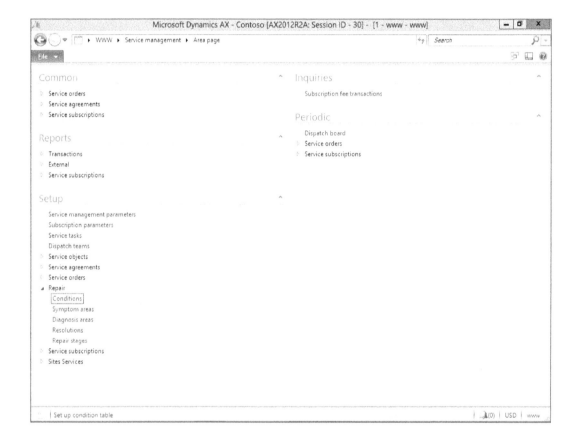

From the **Service management** area page, select the **Conditions** menu item from the **Repair** folder of the **Setup** group.

Defining Repair Conditions

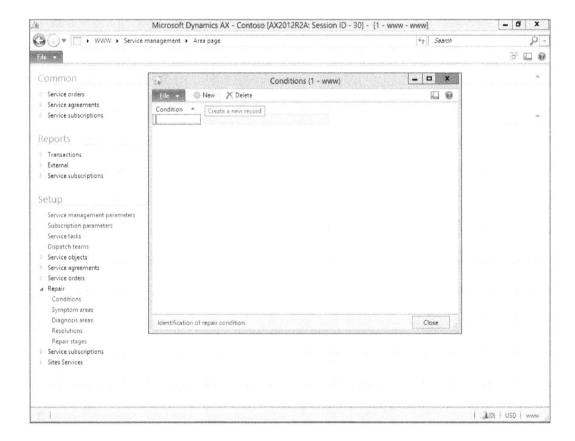

When the **Conditions** maintenance for is displayed, click on the **New** button in the menu bar to create a new **Condition** record.

Defining Repair Conditions

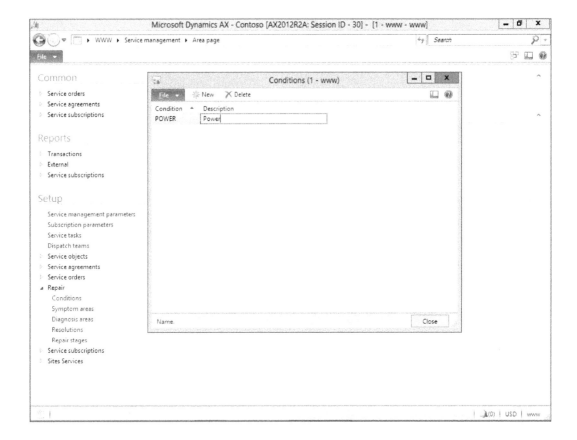

Then add a **Condition** code and a **Description** for the condition.

Defining Repair Conditions

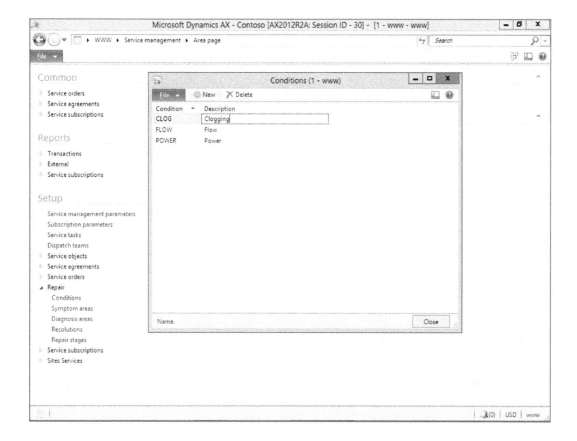

Continue adding **Conditions** and when you have finished, click on the **Close** button to exit the form.

Defining Repair Symptoms & Codes

The next piece of information that you can track on repairs are the **Repair Symptoms**. These are usually the initial symptoms that are reported that initiate the **Service Order**. They may not be the actual cause of the problem, but they may be the most noticeable ones. There can also be two levels to the **Symptoms**, the **Area** which would be where the problem was reported, and also an optional sub-symptom called the **Symptom code** which may describe what was happening to the **Symptom Area.**

Defining Repair Symptoms & Codes

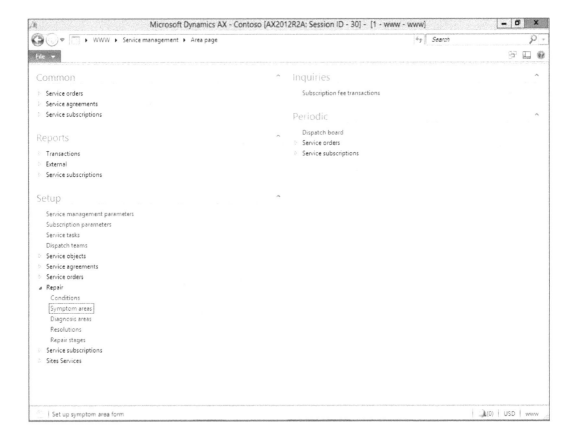

From the **Service management** area page, select the **Symptom areas** menu item from the **Repair** folder of the **Setup** group.

Defining Repair Symptoms & Codes

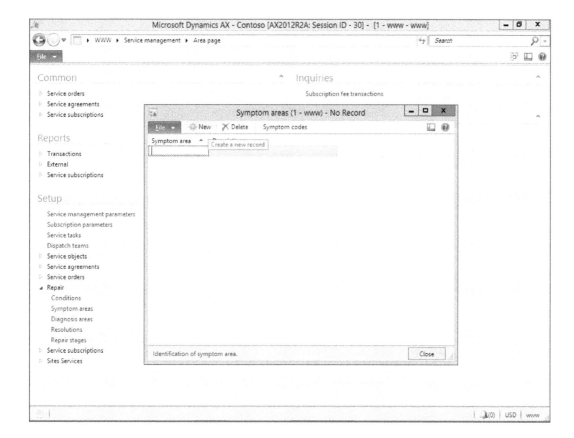

When the **Symptom area** maintenance for is displayed, click on the **New** button in the menu bar to create a new **Symptom area** record.

Defining Repair Symptoms & Codes

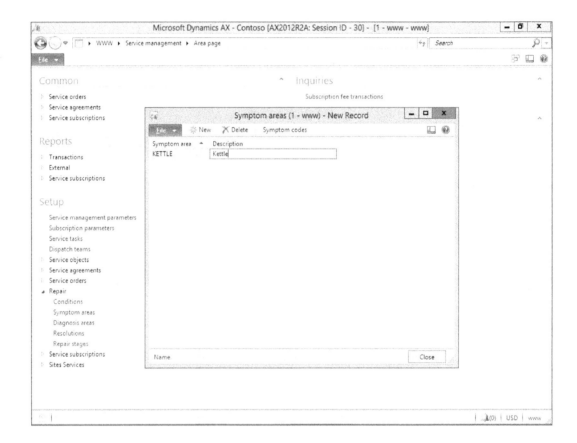

Then add a **Symptom area** code and a **Description** for the condition.

Defining Repair Symptoms & Codes

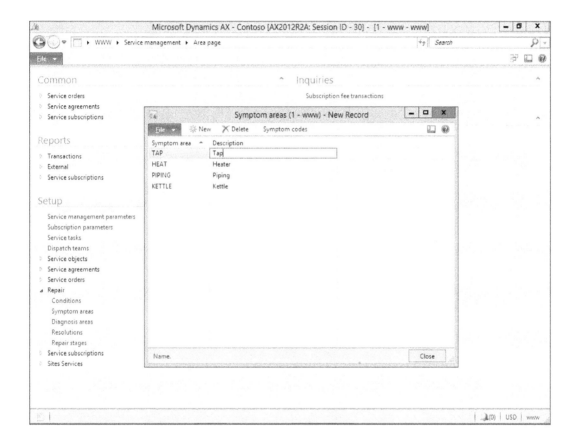

Continue adding **Symptom areas** until you have created them all.

If you want to add more detail to the **Symptom areas** then you can click on the **Symptom codes** menu item to open up the **Symptom codes** maintenance form.

Defining Repair Symptoms & Codes

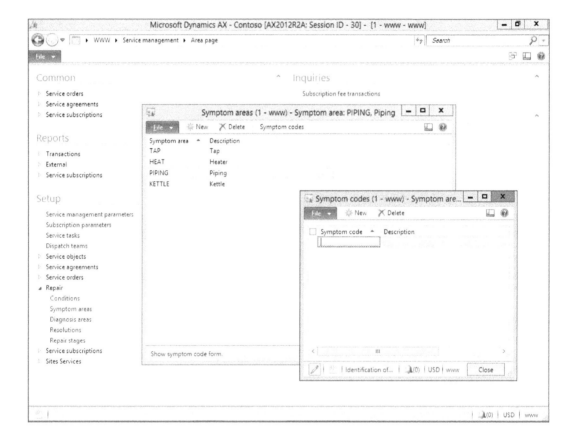

To add a sub-category of the **Symptom code**, click on the **New** button in the menu bar to create a new **Symptom code** record and then add a **Symptom code** and a **Description**.

Defining Repair Symptoms & Codes

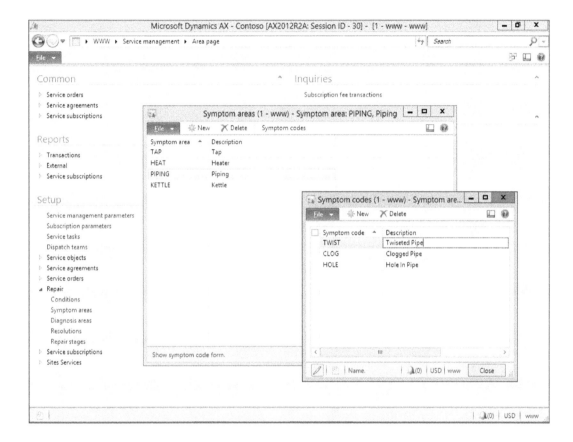

Continue adding you **Symptom codes** and when you have finished, click on the **Close** button to exit the form.

Defining Repair Diagnosis Areas

The **Service Management** area also allows you to track the **Repair Diagnosis** on the **Repair**. These are usually the actual problems diagnosed by the technician during the **Service Order**. There can be two levels to the **Diagnosis**, the **Area** which would be what the problem is, and also an optional **Diagnosis code** which describes how to fix the problem.

In this example we will show how you can configure your own **Diagnosis Areas** and **Diagnosis Codes**.

Defining Repair Diagnosis Areas

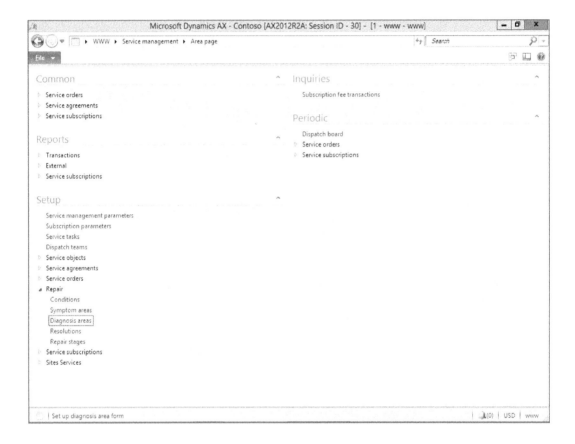

From the **Service management** area page, select the **Diagnosis areas** menu item from the **Repair** folder of the **Setup** group.

Defining Repair Diagnosis Areas

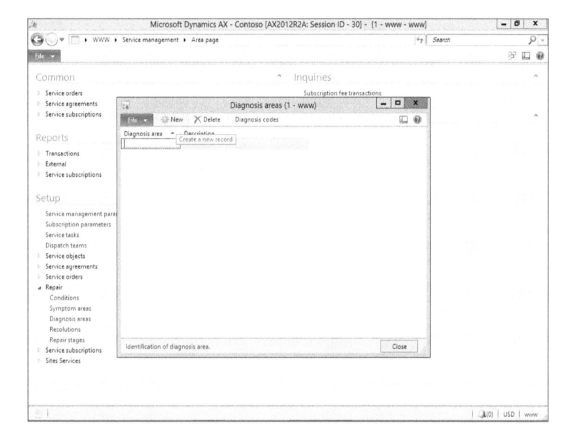

When the **Diagnosis area** maintenance for is displayed, click on the **New** button in the menu bar to create a new **Diagnosis area** record.

Defining Repair Diagnosis Areas

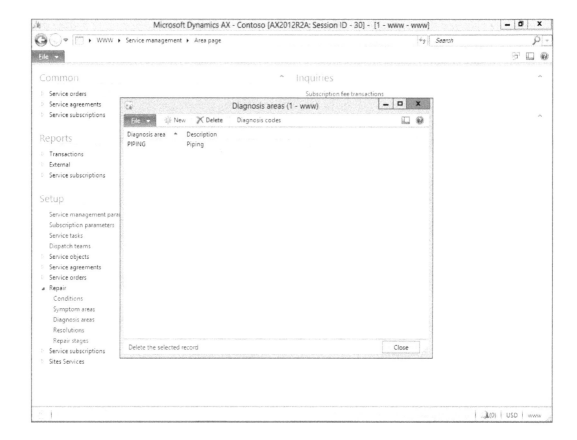

Then add a **Diagnosis area** code and a **Description**.

Defining Repair Diagnosis Areas

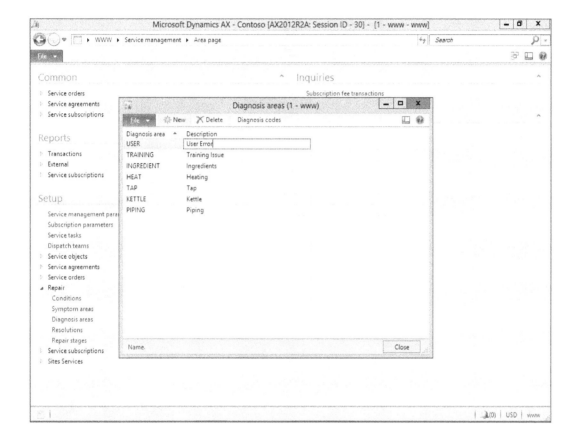

Continue adding **Diagnosis areas** until you have created them all.

Defining Repair Diagnoses & Resolution

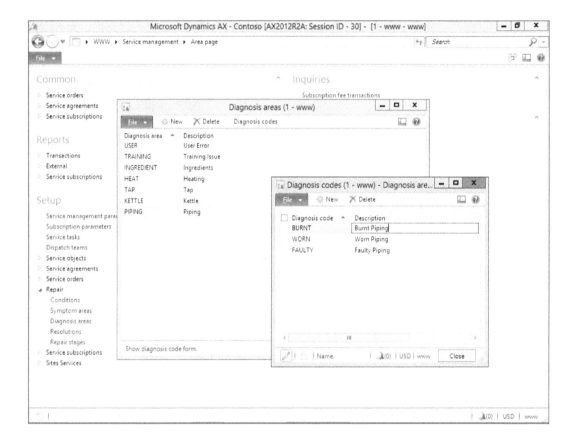

If you want to add more detail to the **Diagnosis areas** then you can click on the **Diagnosis codes** menu item to open up the **Diagnosis codes** maintenance form.

To add a sub-category of the **Diagnosis code**, click on the **New** button in the menu bar to create a new **Diagnosis code** record and then add a **Diagnosis code** and a **Description**.

Continue adding you **Diagnosis codes** and when you have finished, click on the **Close** button to exit the form.

Defining Repair Resolutions

The final piece of information that you can configure to track the repairs is the **Repair Resolution**. This is used to track what was done to complete the repair, and you can use it for reporting and analysis.

On this example we will show how you can configure your own **Repair Resolution** codes.

Defining Repair Resolutions

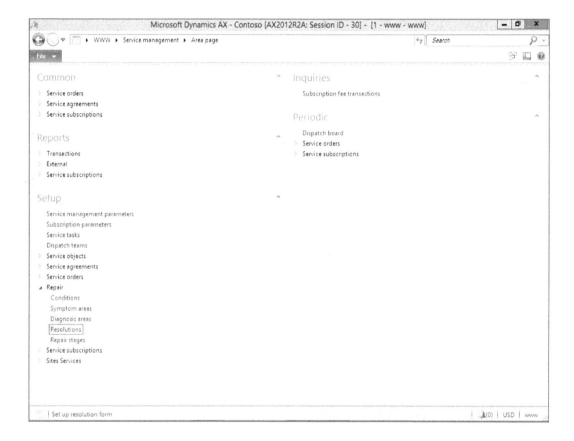

From the **Service management** area page, select the **Resolutions** menu item from the **Repair** folder of the **Setup** group.

Defining Repair Resolutions

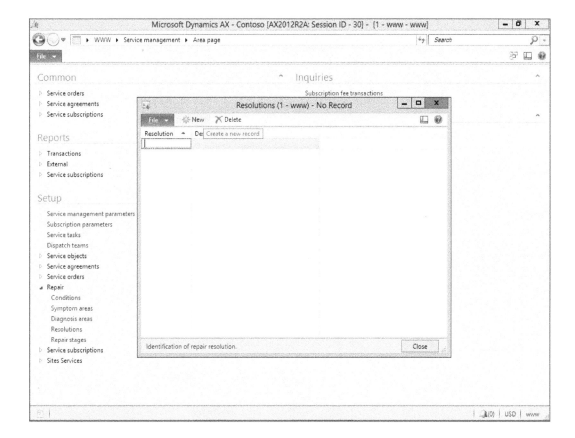

When the **Resolutions** maintenance for is displayed, click on the **New** button in the menu bar to create a new **Resolution** record.

Defining Repair Resolutions

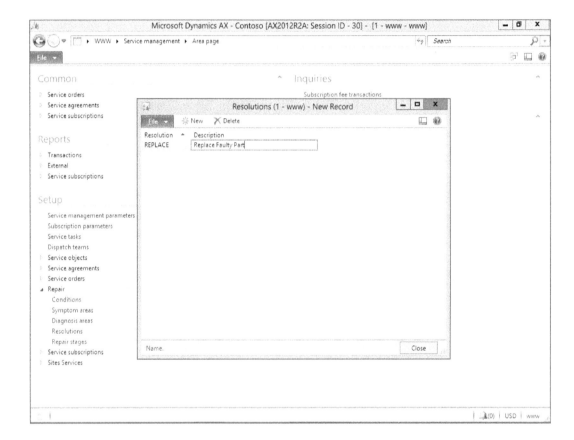

Then add a **Resolution** code and a **Description** for the condition.

Defining Repair Diagnoses & Resolution

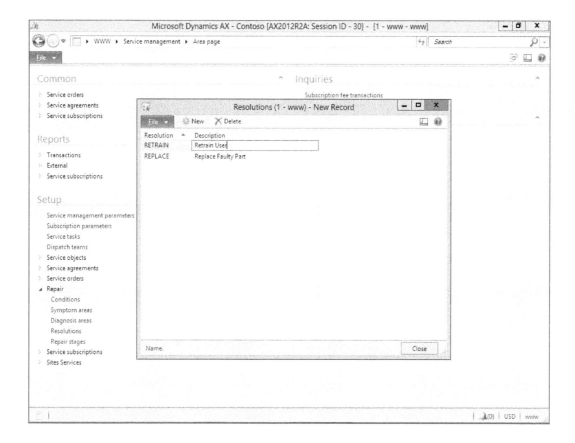

Continue adding **Resolutions** and when you have finished, click on the **Close** button to exit the form.

Defining Repair Stages

If you want to, you also have the option to track the **Repair Stages**, so that you can track the progress of repairs.

In this example we will show how you can configure your own **Repair Stages**.

Defining Repair Stages

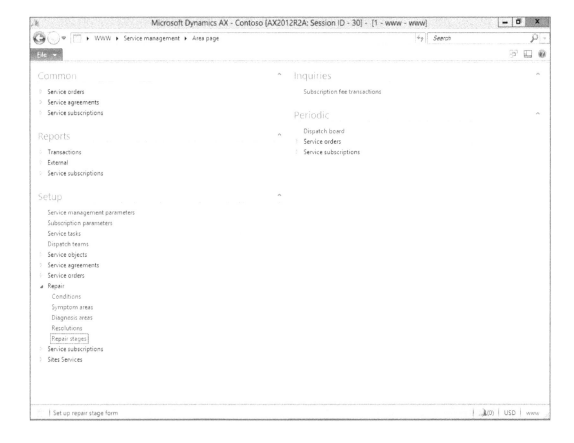

From the **Service management** area page, select the **Repair stage** menu item from the **Repair** folder of the **Setup** group.

Defining Repair Stages

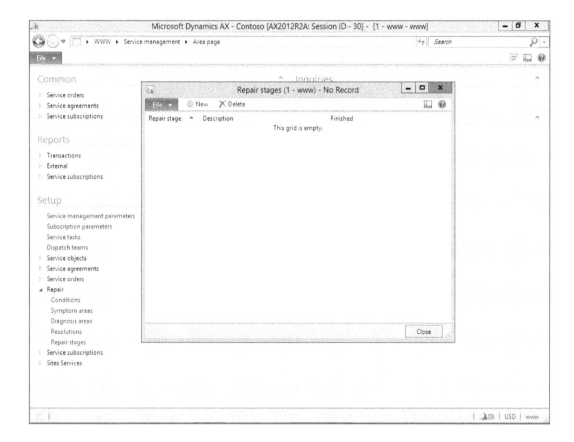

When the **Repair stages** maintenance for is displayed, click on the **New** button in the menu bar to create a new **Repair stage** record.

Defining Repair Stages

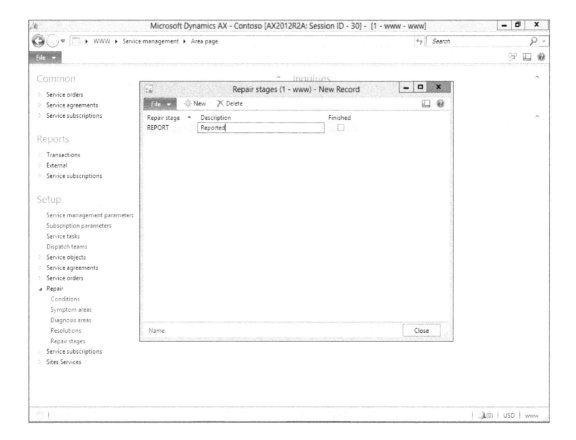

Then add a **Repair stage** code, a **Description** for the condition, and if the stage is the end of the process, then check the **Finished** check box.

Defining Repair Stages

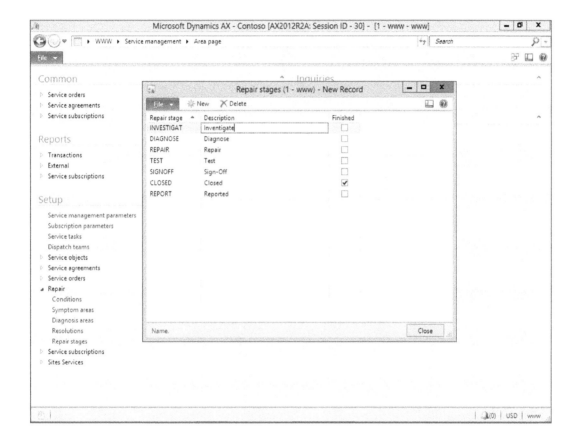

Continue adding **Repair stages** and when you have finished, click on the **Close** button to exit the form.

Recording Repair Operations

Once all of the codes have been configured for your **Repair** process, you can now start tracking the repairs against **Service Orders** and **Agreements**. This is a great way to track what has been done in the past, and also if a **Service Order** is being continually raised against a **Service Agreement** or a **Service Object** then you can start tracking if the resolutions for the repairs are actually working.

In this example we will show how the **Repair** tracking process works.

Recording Repair Operations

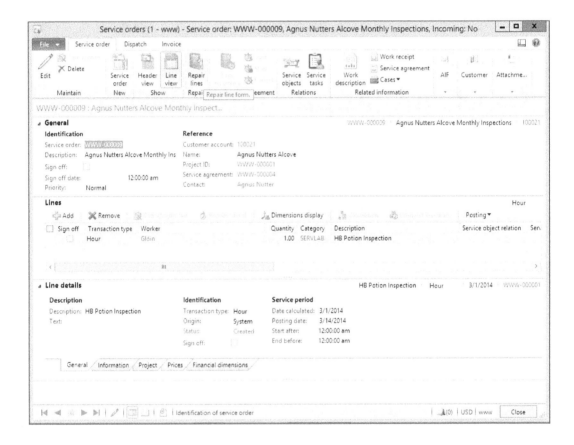

To start the **Repair** tracking process, select your **Service Order** that you are working on, and then click the **Repair lines** button within the **Repair** group of the **Service Orders** ribbon bar.

Recording Repair Operations

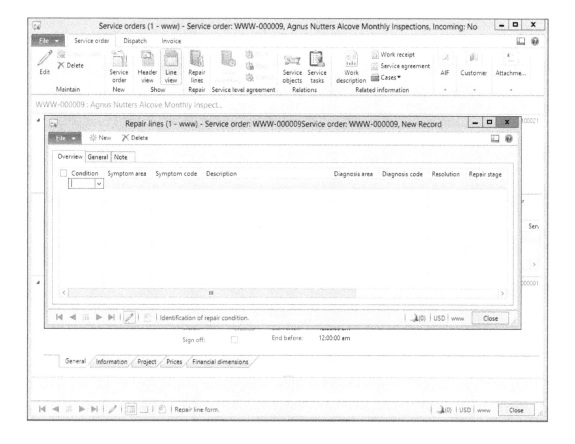

When the **Repair Lines** maintenance form is displayed, click the **New** button in the menu bar to create a new **Repair** record.

Recording Repair Operations

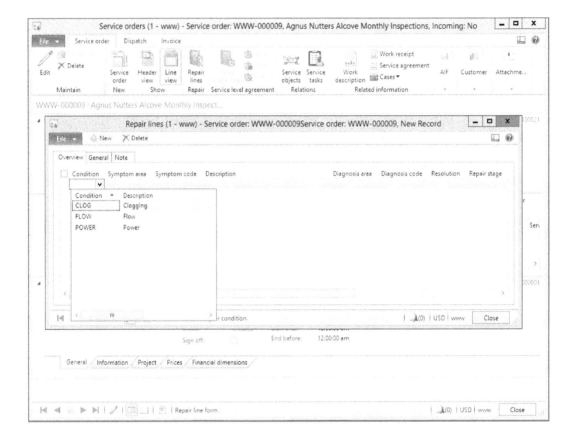

Select the **Condition** (the general problem) from the drop down list.

Recording Repair Operations

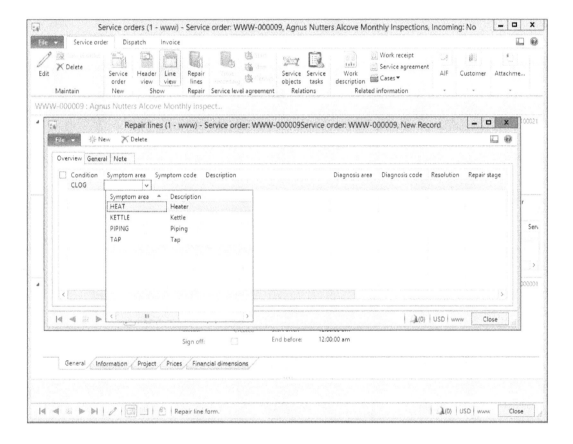

If you know the area that the problem is being reported to happen then you can select it form the **Symptom area** drop down box.

Recording Repair Operations

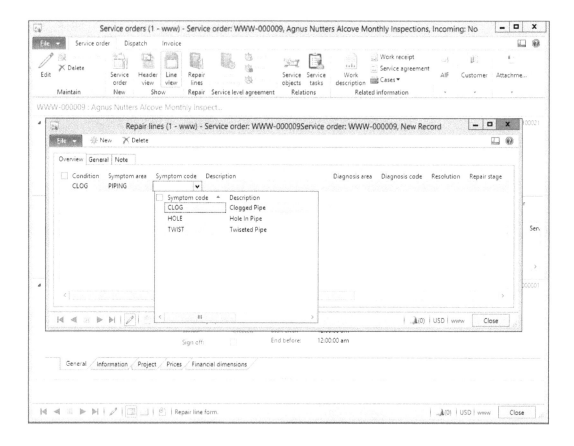

If you have additional details about the **Symptom**, then you can also select it from the **Symptom code** drop down list.

Recording Repair Operations

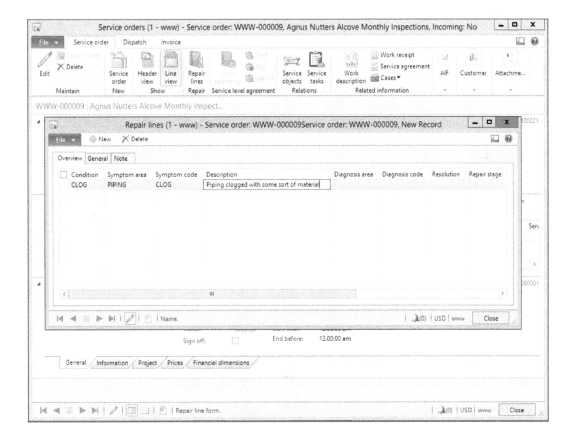

In the **Description** field, enter in a brief description of the problem.

Recording Repair Operations

If you have a more detailed description, then select the **Note** tab, and you will be able to enter a virtually unlimited number of lines in the **Text** field.

Recording Repair Operations

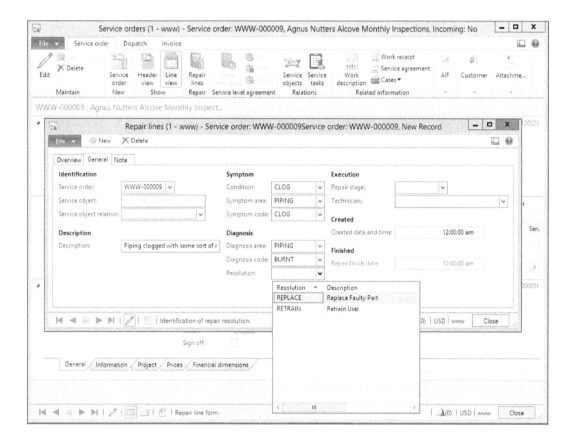

As more information is gathered on the **Repair** then you can also update the **Diagnosis area**, the **Diagnosis code**, and the **Resolution.**

When you have finished updating the **Repair** click the **Close** button to exit out of the form.

Recording Repair Operations

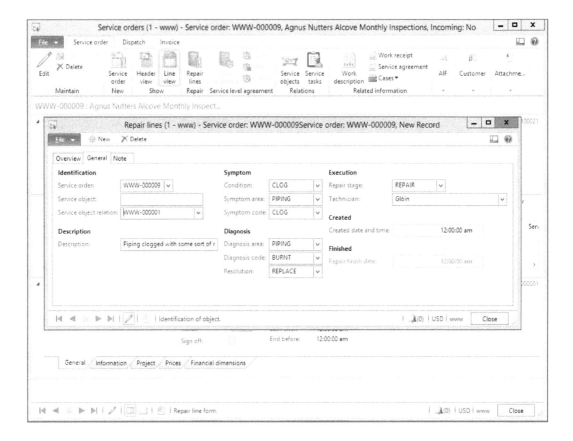

Also you can specify the **Service Object Relation** for the repair line so that the repair is linked with the **Service Objects**.

When you are done, just click on the **Close** button to exit from the form and return to the **Service Order**.

DISPATCH TEAMS

If you want to further organize your **Service Management**, then you can group your **Service Technicians** into **Dispatch Teams**, and then schedule them through the dispatching workbench. The bonus is that it doesn't take much work to get this configured either,

Configuring Dispatch Teams

The first step in the process is to create your **Dispatch Teams** within Dynamics AX. This will be used to group your service technicians together, and also to make sure they show up on the **Dispatch Workbench**.

Configuring Dispatch Teams

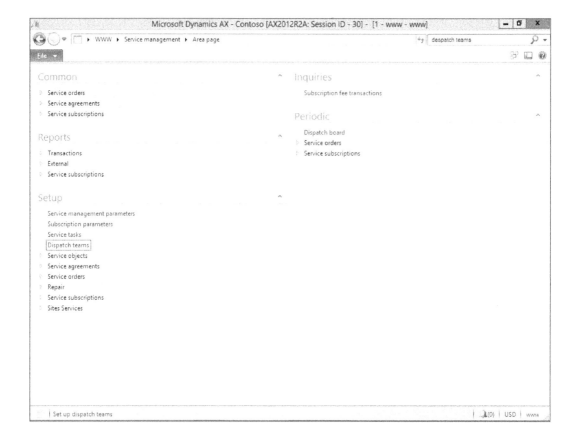

Click on the **Dispatch Teams** menu item within the **Setup** group of the **Service Management** area page.

Configuring Dispatch Teams

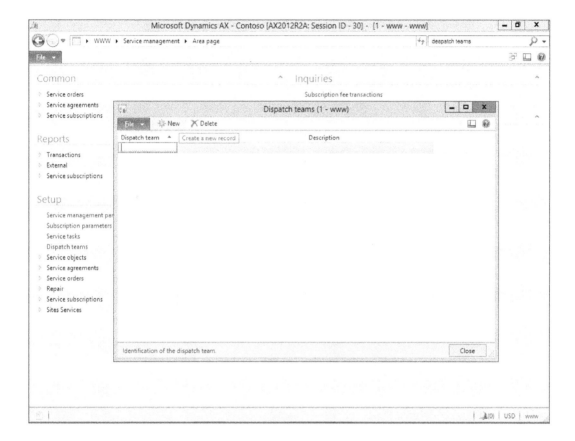

When the **Dispatch Teams** maintenance form is displayed, click on the **New** button in the menu bar to create a new record.

Configuring Dispatch Teams

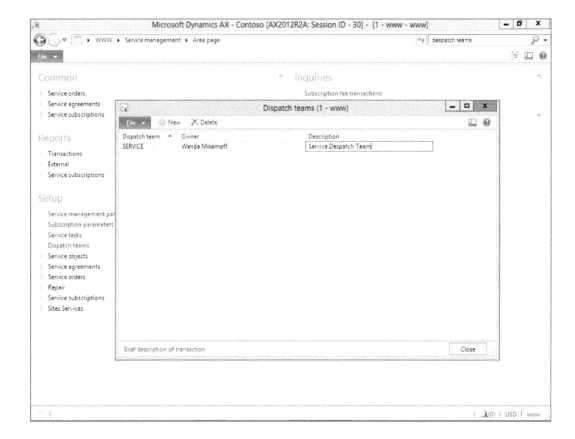

Then assign a code to the **Dispatch Team**, assign a worker as the **Owner** of the team, and then give your team a **Description**.

Repeat the process for each Dispatch team,. And when you are done, click on the **Close** button to exit from the form.

Assigning Workers To Dispatch Teams

Once you have a **Dispatch Team**, you need to assign your technicians to it so that they will show up on the **Dispatch Workbench**.

Assigning Workers To Dispatch Teams

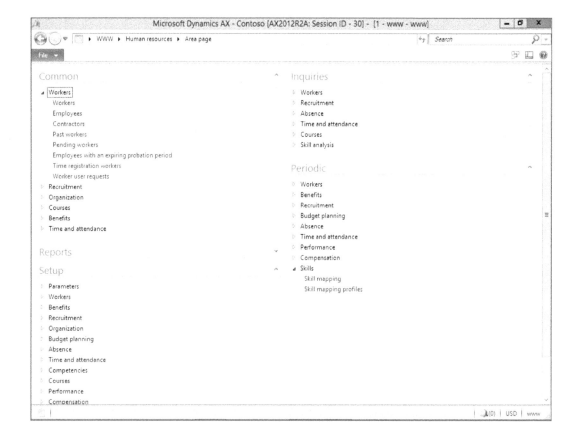

Click on the **Workers** menu item within the **Workers** folder of the **Common** group of the **Human Resources** area page.

Assigning Workers To Dispatch Teams

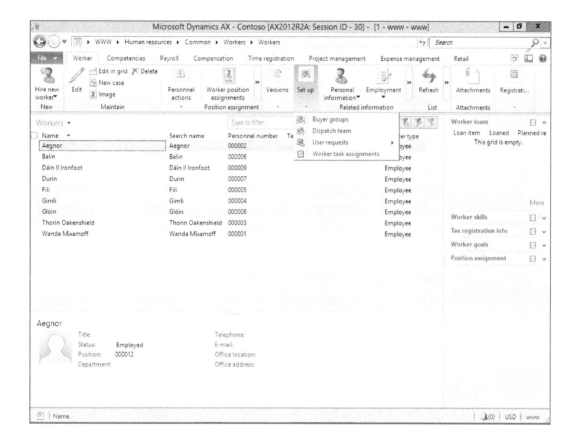

When the **Worker** list page is displayed, select the **Worker** that you want to add to the **Dispatch Team**, and then click on the **Dispatch Team** menu item within the **Setup** group of the **Worker** ribbon bar.

Assigning Workers To Dispatch Teams

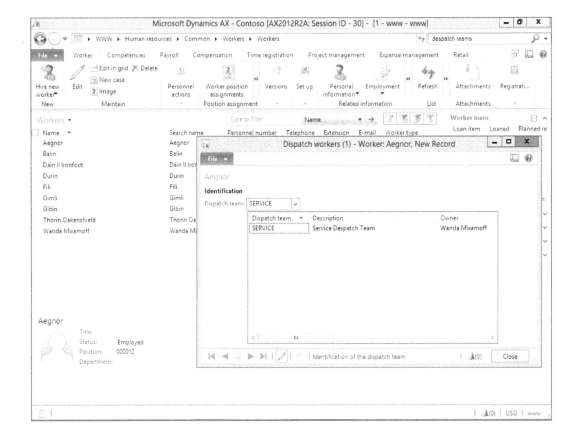

When the **Dispatch Workers** maintenance form is displayed, select the **Dispatch Team** from the dropdown box, and click the **Close** button to exit the form.

Viewing Service Orders In The Dispatch Board

Now that you have the Dispatch Teams configured, you can now see them on the **Dispatch Board**.

Viewing Service Orders In The Dispatch Board

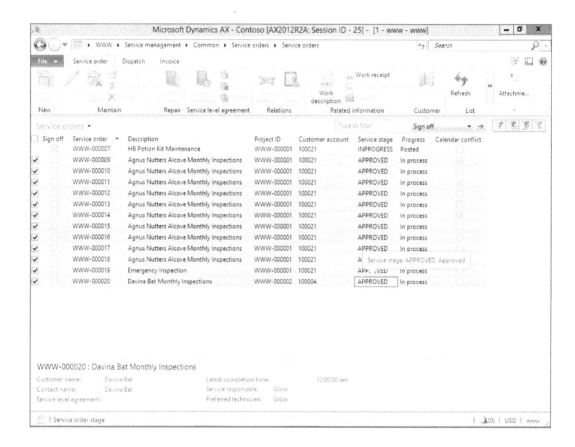

Before you start though you need to have the Service Orders that you want to dispatch in a stage that has a Dispatch Activity created against it. In the Service Management Parameters there was an option that specified when that stage was.

Viewing Service Orders In The Dispatch Board

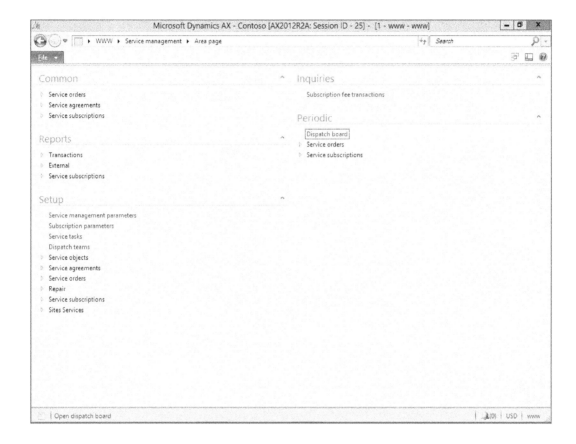

To see the **Dispatch Board** click on the **Dispatch Board** menu item within the **Periodic** group of the **Service Management** area page.

Viewing Service Orders In The Dispatch Board

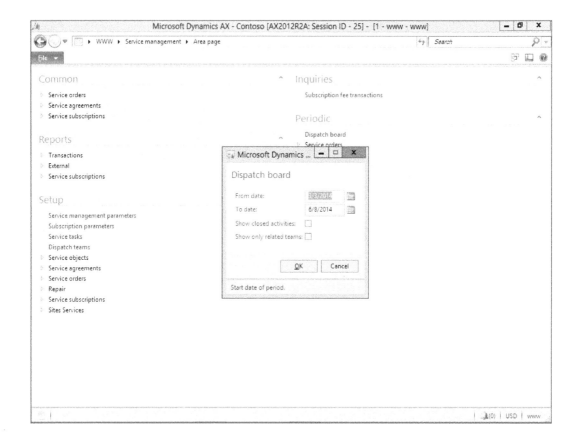

When the **Dispatch Board** dialog box is displayed, select the date range that you want to see all of the Service Orders within and then click on the **OK** button.

Note: The to and from dates are defaulted in from the Service Management Parameters

Viewing Service Orders In The Dispatch Board

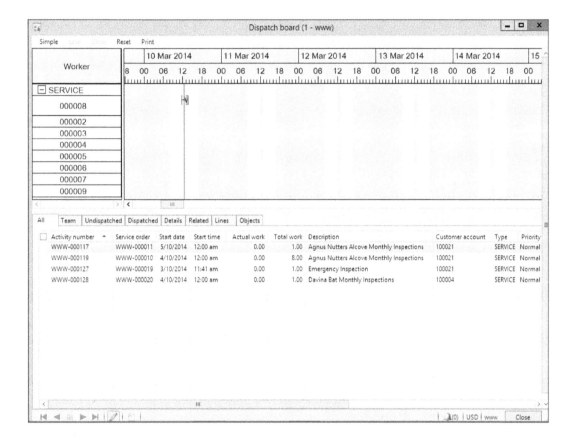

When the **Dispatch Board** is displayed, you will see all of the members of the **Dispatch Team** and a Gantt chart that shows all of the **Service Orders.**

From here you can move the service orders within the schedule, and also assign them to other Technicians just by dragging them to the other rows.

Viewing Service Orders In The Dispatch Board

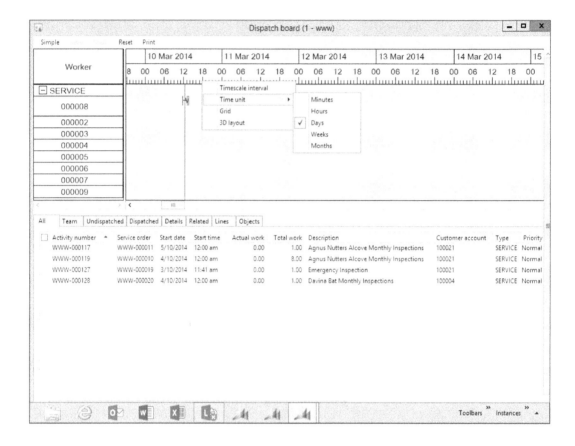

Tip: If you right-mouse-click on the timeline you will be able to change the Time Unit of the Gantt chart.

Viewing Service Orders In The Dispatch Board

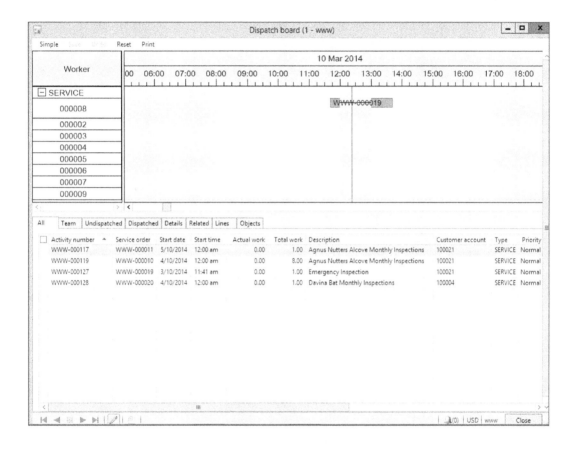

This will make it easier to see the actual Service Orders.

When you are done, just click on the **Close** button to exit from the form.

SERVICE SUBSCRIPTIONS

The final area of the **Service Management** module that we will look at is the **Service Subscriptions** feature. This allows you to automatically create periodic subscription fees for Customers that then move through to be invoiced just like the **Service Order** transactions. The major difference is that there are no Service Orders generated for these fees.

Configuring Subscription Groups

The first step in the process is to create your **Subscription Groups** that will allow you to segregate your Subscriptions for updates and reporting.

Configuring Subscription Groups

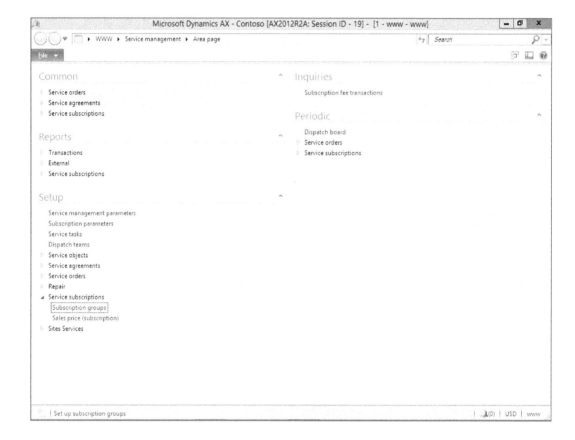

To do this, click on the **Subscription Groups** menu item within the **Service Subscriptions** folder of the **Setup** group within the **Service Management** area page.

Configuring Subscription Groups

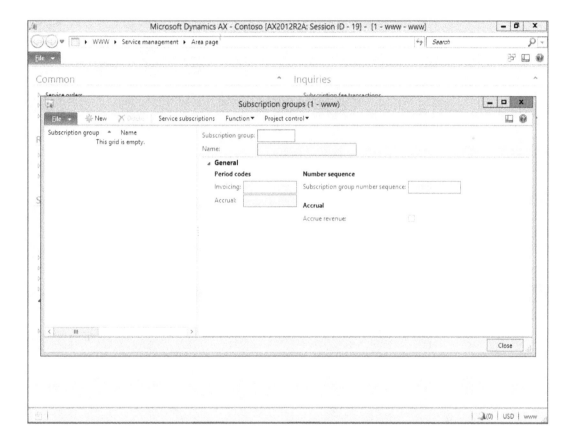

When the **Subscription Groups** maintenance form is displayed, click on the **New** button within the menu bar to create a new record.

Configuring Subscription Groups

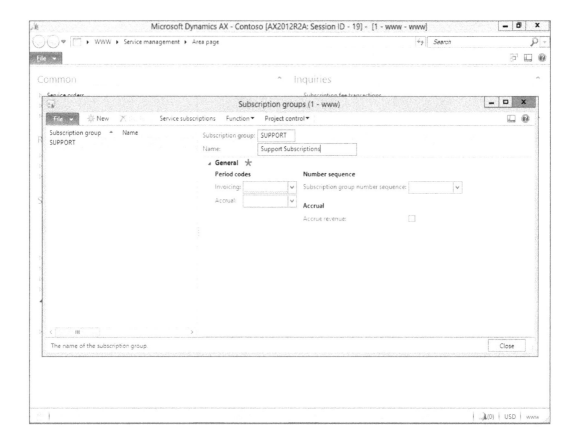

Assign a code to the **Subscription Group**, and also give it a **Description.**

Configuring Subscription Groups

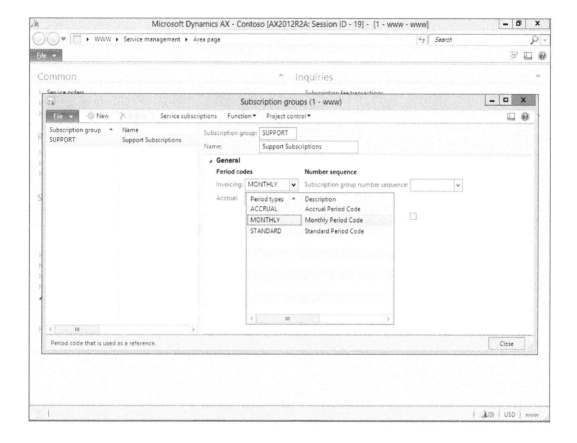

Select a period code from the **Invoicing** drop down list. This will be the frequency that you will use for the creation of the **Service Subscriptions**.

Configuring Subscription Groups

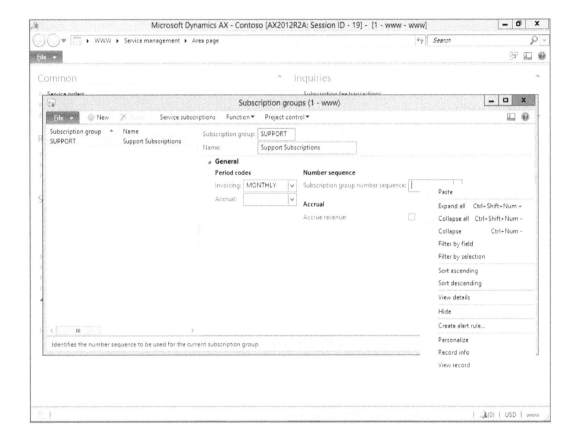

If you do not already have a number sequence defined for your **Subscription Group Number Sequence**, then right-mouse click on the field and select the **View Details** option.

Configuring Subscription Groups

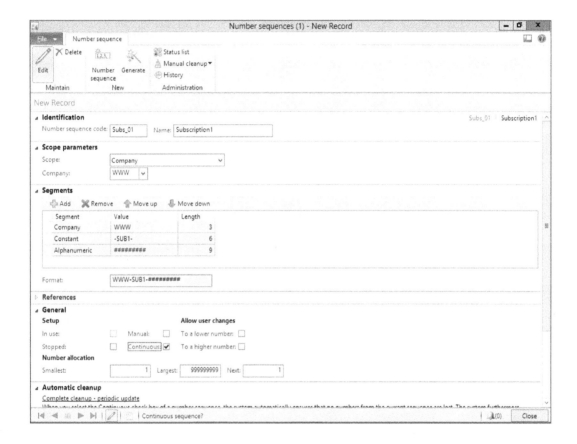

When the **Number Sequence** maintenance form is displayed, create a new record and numbering definition, and then click the **Close** button to exit from the form.

Configuring Subscription Groups

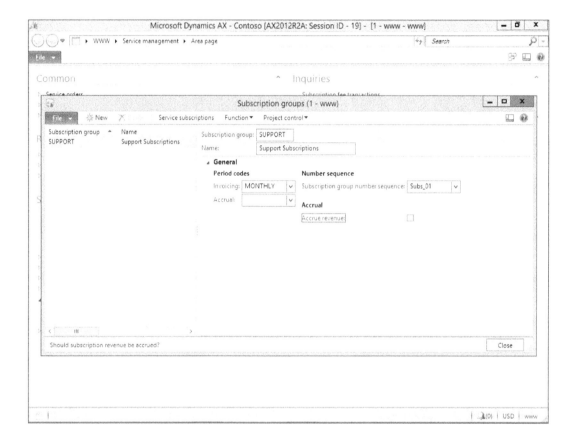

Then set the **Subscription Group Number Sequence**.

Continue adding additional **Subscription Groups**, and when you are done, click on the **Close** button to exit from the form.

Creating Service Subscriptions

Now you can create your **Service Subscription** templates.

Creating Service Subscriptions

Click on the **All Service Subscriptions** menu item from within the **Service Subscriptions** folder of the **Common** group of the **Service Management** area page.

Creating Service Subscriptions

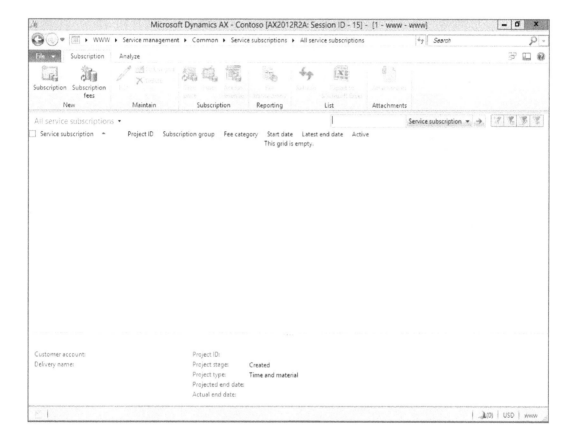

When the **Service Subscriptions** list page is displayed, click on the **Subscription** button within the **New** group of the **Subscription** ribbon bar.

Creating Service Subscriptions

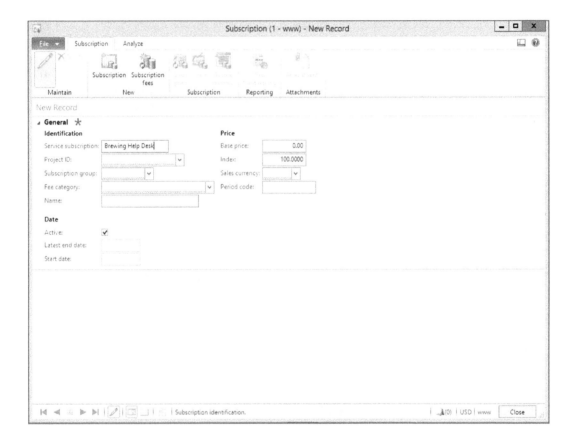

When the **Subscription** maintenance form is displayed, give it a description in the **Service Subscription** field.

Creating Service Subscriptions

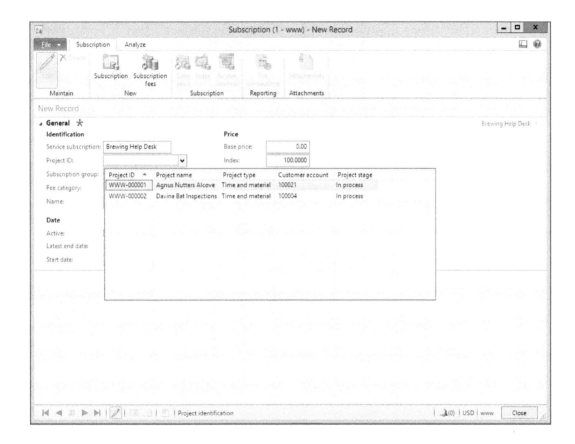

Then select the **Project ID** that you want to associate with the **Service Subscription.**

Creating Service Subscriptions

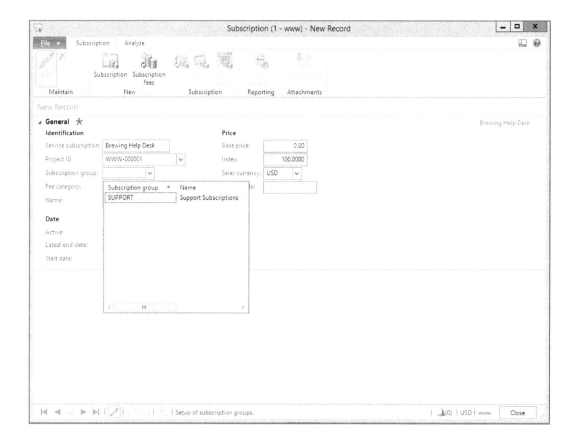

From the **Subscription Group** dropdown, select the group that you want to associate with it.

Creating Service Subscriptions

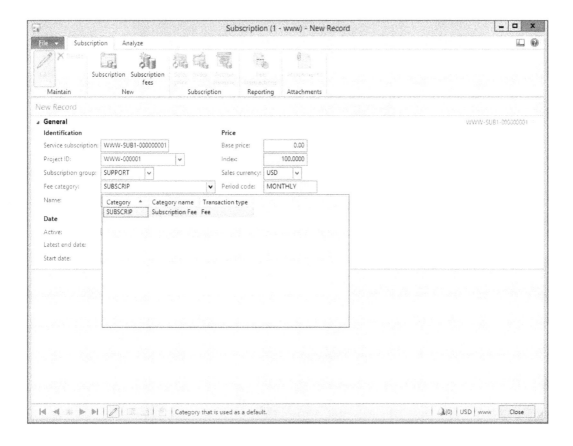

Select the **Fee Category** that you want to use when the **Subscription Fee** is generated.

Creating Service Subscriptions

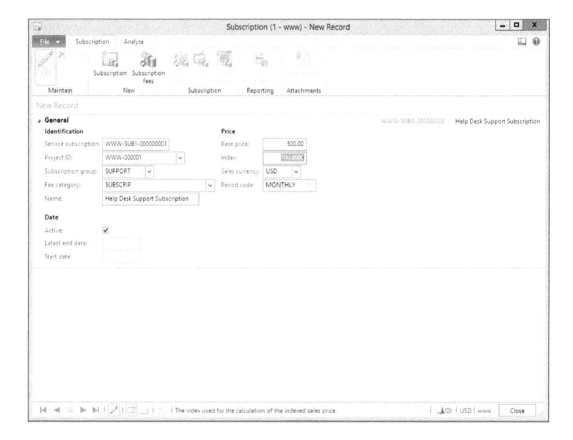

And then select the **Base Price** that you want to charge for the fee.

Creating Service Subscriptions

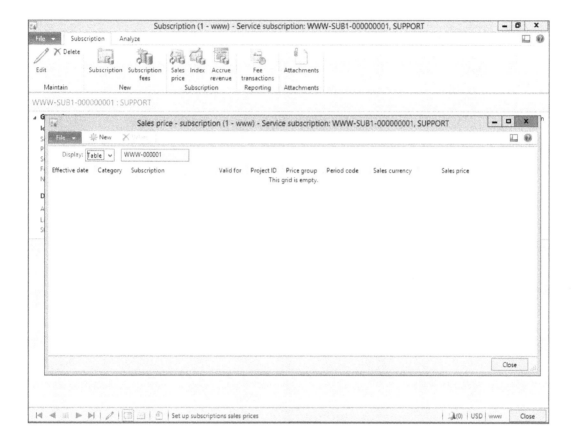

If you want to have more elaborate pricing for the fee, then click on the **Sales Price** menu item within the **Subscription** group of the **Subscription** ribbon bar.

To add a new record, just click on the **New** button within the menu bar.

Creating Service Subscriptions

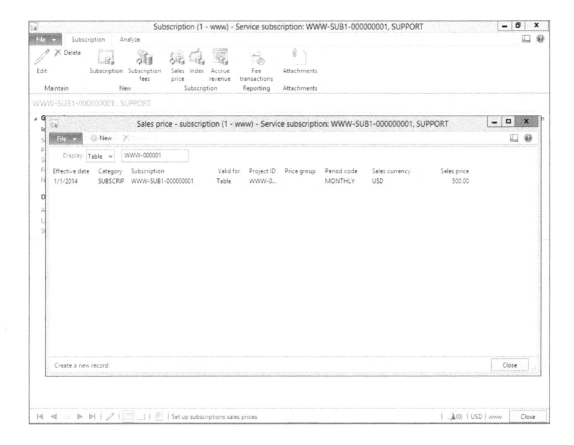

This will allow you to enter price records for the Subscription with different **Sales Prices** and also **Effective Dates**.

Creating Service Subscriptions

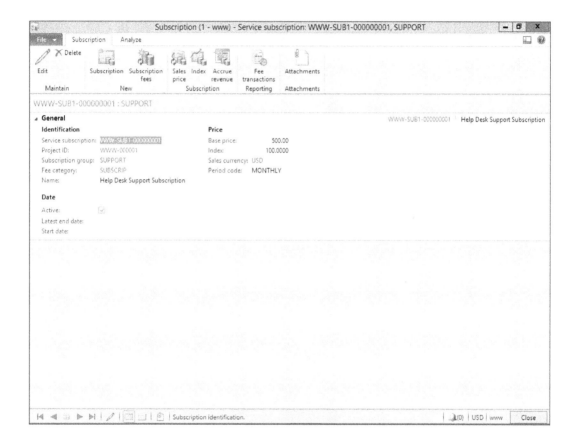

When you are done, just click on the **Close** button to exit from the form.

Creating Service Subscriptions

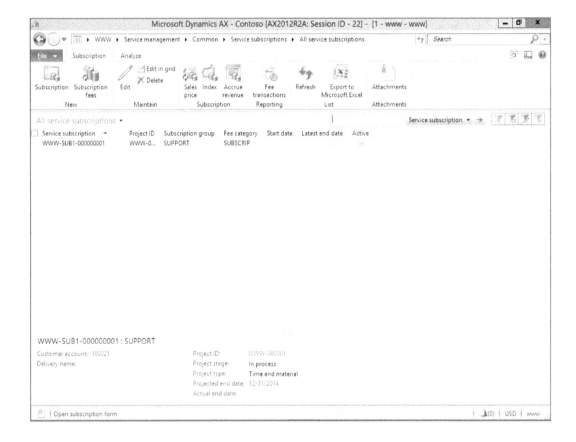

Now you should have a **Service Subscription** ready for billing.

Generating Subscription Fees

Once you have defined all of your **Service Subscriptions**, you can get Dynamics AX to create the Fee transactions for you.

Generating Subscription Fees

To do this, select the **Subscription Fee** record that you want to generate the fees for, and click on the **Subscription Fee** button within the **New** group **of the** Subscription **ribbon bar.**

Generating Subscription Fees

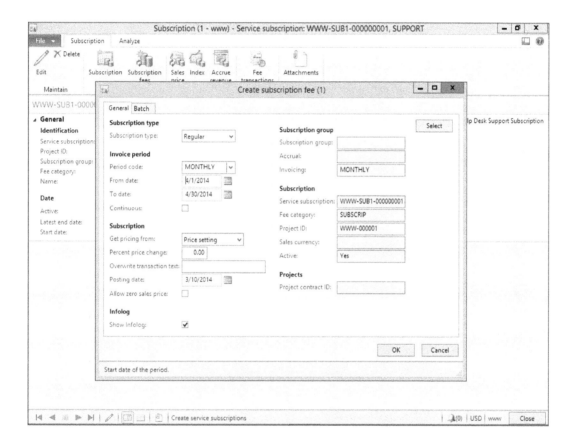

When the **Create Subscription Fee** dialog box is displayed, select the **From** and **To Date** that you want to generate over, and click on the **OK** button.

Generating Subscription Fees

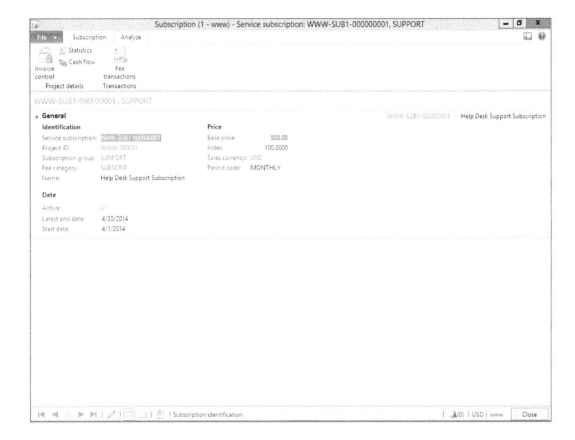

When you return to the **Service Subscription** to see the fees that have been generated, just click on **Fee Transactions** menu button within the **Transactions** group of the **Analyze** ribbon bar.

Generating Subscription Fees

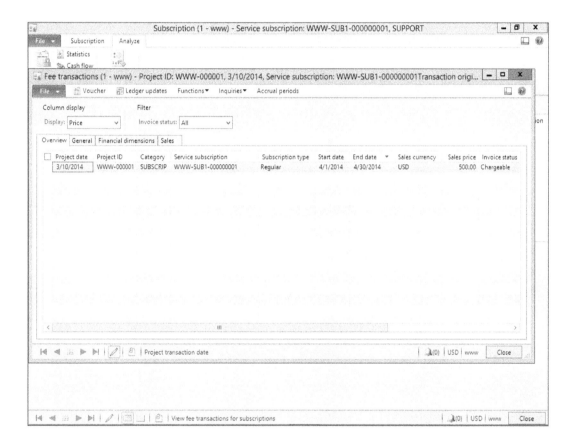

You should see that the fees for the **Subscription** have been created.

Creating Fee Transaction In Mass

Rather than creating the Fees one at a time from the **Subscription**, you can create them in mass, gathering up everything that needs to be billed within a certain time frame.

Creating Fee Transaction In Mass

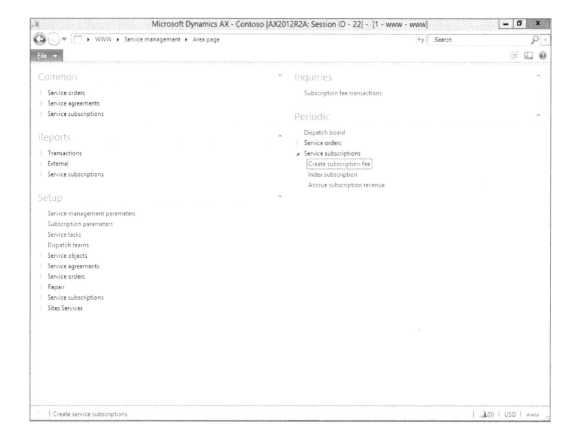

Click on the **Create Subscription Fee** menu item within the **Service Subscriptions** folder of the **Periodic** group of the **Service Management** area page.

Creating Fee Transaction In Mass

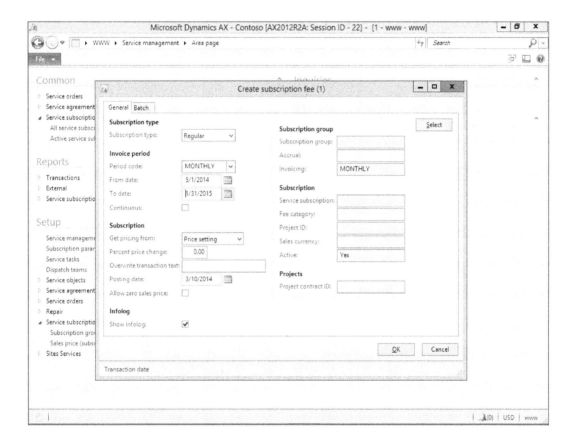

When the **Create Subscription Fee** dialog box is displayed, select the **From** and **To Date** that you want to generate over, and click on the **OK** button.

Reviewing Fee Transactions

Once you have created all of your Subscription Fees, you can easily review them just to make sure that they are all correct.

Reviewing Fee Transactions

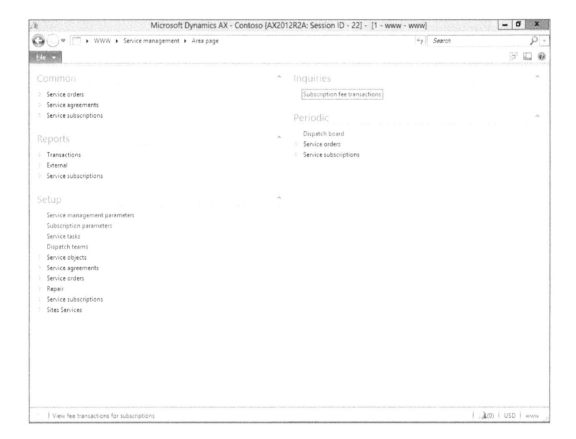

To do this, click on the **Subscription Fee Transactions** menu item within the **Inquiries** group of the **Service Management** area page.

Reviewing Fee Transactions

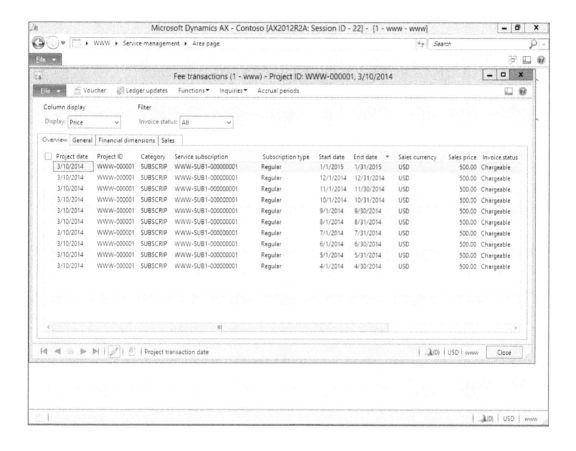

This will show you the **Fee Transactions** that you have created.

Creating Invoice Proposals For Subscription Fees

Once the **Subscription Fees** have been created, all that is left for you to do is to post them and invoice the customers.

Creating Invoice Proposals For Subscription Fees

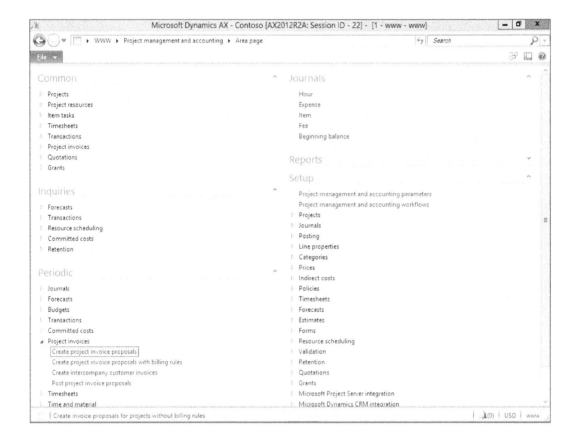

To do that, click on the **Create Project Invoice Proposals** menu item within the **Project Invoices** folder of the **Periodic** group within **Project Management and Accounting**.

Creating Invoice Proposals For Subscription Fees

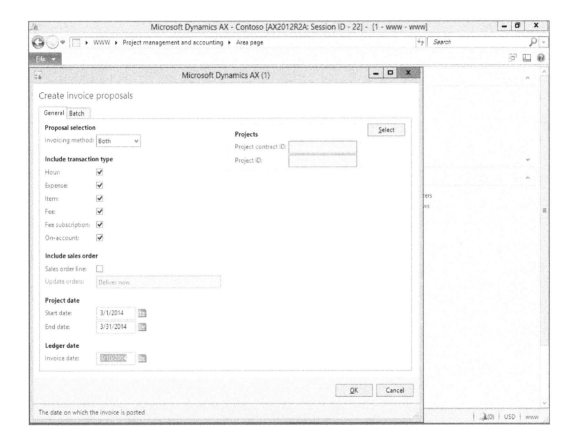

When the **Create Invoice Proposals** dialog box is displayed, select the date range that you want to invoice, and also the **Invoice Date** that you would like to use, and then click the **OK** button.

Creating Invoice Proposals For Subscription Fees

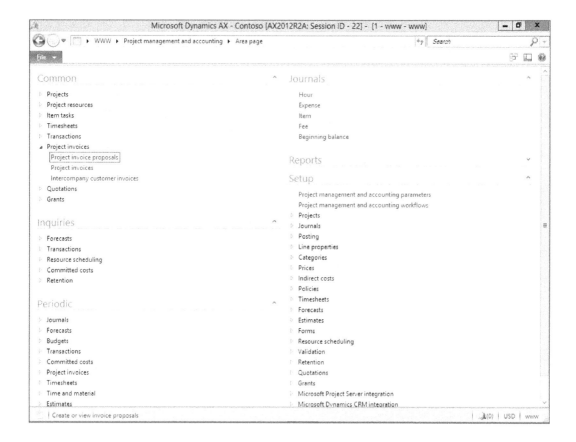

To view the invoices, click on the **Project Invoice Proposals** menu button within the **Project Invoices** folder of the **Common** group within the **Project Management and Accounting** area page.

Creating Invoice Proposals For Subscription Fees

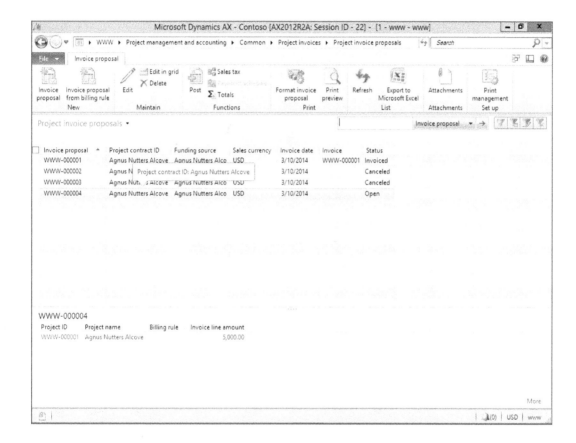

When the **Project Invoice Proposals** list page is displayed, you can drill into any of the **Invoice Proposals**.

Creating Invoice Proposals For Subscription Fees

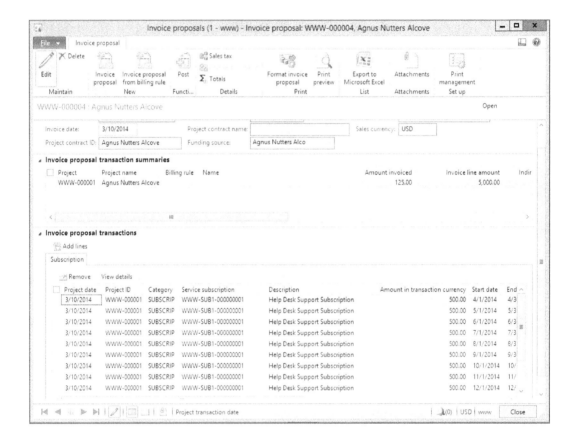

This will show you the Invoice Proposal, along with all the Subscription Fees that are associated with it.

To invoice the fees, just click the **Post** button within the **Functions** group of the **Invoice Proposals** ribbon bar.

When you are done, just click on the **Close** button to exit.

Summary

In this blueprint we have shown a number of the features that you can easily take advantage of within the **Service Management** area of Dynamics AX. By leveraging the **Project accounting** area, the **Service Management** functions give you a lot of power without having to invest a lot of effort in the setup.

You can use many of these features to track both external and internal service projects, so you may want to try using this for:

• Customer Service Orders (as we have shown in this example)

• Simple internal maintenance repair operations

• Help desk support tracking

Additionally, there are features that we did not describe in the walk through that you may want to investigate. They include:

• Sourcing repair items from inventory

• Creation of Service Orders from projects

Take a look at the **Service Management** module, it's simple to configure, and could help a lot.

About the Author

Murray Fife is a Microsoft Dynamics AX MVP, author of Extending Dynamics AX 2012 Cookbook, and Solution Architect at I.B.I.S. Inc with over 18 years of experience in the software industry.

Like most people in this industry he has paid his dues as a developer, an implementation consultant, a trainer, and now spend most of his days working with companies solving their problems with the Microsoft suite of products, specializing in the Dynamics® AX solutions.

Founded in 1989, I.B.I.S., Inc. (www.ibisinc.com) provides distributors and manufacturers with next-generation supply chain solutions to maximize their profitability. A winning combination of industry and supply chain expertise, world-class supply chain software developed in partnership with distributors and manufacturers, and 25 years of successful Microsoft Dynamics implementations has culminated in making I.B.I.S., Inc. the preferred Microsoft Dynamics partner and solution provider for distributors and manufacturers worldwide.

EMAIL	murray@murrayfife.me
TWITTER	@murrayfife
SKYPE	murrayfife
AMAZON	http://www.amazon.com/author/murrayfife
BLOG	http://dynamicsaxtipoftheday.com
	http://extendingdynamicsax.com
	http://atinkerersnotebook.com
SLIDESHARE	http://slideshare.net/murrayfife
LINKEDIN	http://www.linkedin.com/in/murrayfife

www.ingramcontent.com/pod-product-compliance
Lightning Source LLC
Chambersburg PA
CBHW080141060326
40689CB00018B/3811